THE ETERNAL DESTINY SERIES
BOOK TWO

THE BATTLE
for the SEED

THE LOST HISTORY AND THE SAVED RACE

CHRIS & GUY
PAGANO

INKS & BINDINGS

Inks and Bindings
888-290-5218
www.inksandbindings.com
orders@inksandbindings.com

CONTENTS

FOREWORD

By Pastor Mark Zelewicz Sr. lead pastor Relevant Worship Center.

Chris and Guy Pagano catapult the reader into historical scriptures with incredible imagery and characterizations, that speak of the early formation of the world. The Battle For The Seed: The lost history and the saved race, allows the reader to recognize that the same forces of evil that were at work in the beginning are at work against God's people today. Their story will entertain you, enlighten you, challenge you and leave you wanting more! The Battle For The Seed: The lost history and the saved race, is not only a story that will take the reader away from their daily routine but will also guide them into their own findings through questions and references to be used as personal or group bible study tools. I know that every person that reads The Battle For The Seed: The lost history and the saved race, will enjoy this 2nd book by Chris Pagano and Guy Pagano. I am proud to call myself Pastor to these talented, gifted and Spirit led men of God.

PREFACE

Chris and Guy Pagano have read the story of the first family and have believed that there are many worth-while lessons to be learned from those abbreviated accounts. Many people simply skim over these stories, if they read them at all, and many preachers rarely bring these biblical passages to the pulpits. Did this ancient history really happen the way it is portrayed in this novel, or should you the reader consider it nothing more than biblical fiction? Either way, once you have read their account of what they think happened, your appreciation of that genealogy will grow. You will never view the story of Noah and the arc the same again.

CHAPTER ONE

C ain stepped back from his brother as he dropped toward him. Staring down at Abel lying at his feet, Cain's face was frozen with a look of stunned disbelief. His brother's lifeless eyes were open as they faced up into the heavens. Cain noticed what appeared to be a faint smile as the corners of Abel's mouth were turned slightly upward. "No that couldn't be a smile, he said to himself, that had to hurt."

The rest of Abel's body lay motionless and told a contrary reality. It seemed to be expressing wretched horror over what his brother had just done to him.

Before he lost all consciousness Abel turned to look at his assailant with an expression of revulsion draped across his face at the realization: *My own brother did this to me?* then he slumped to the dusty ground. He spoke no words but the body language of his final resting position unnerved Cain. It wasn't just what Cain did that caused Abel's body to look that way. The manner with which he killed him, like a stealthy cat seizing upon its prey was inexplicable. That he did it at all, with his own bloody hands, was especially appalling and without excuse. Nothing like this had ever been done before. Cain knew that no one has ever taken the life of another, especially that of his own beloved brother. He continued to stare down at him, *is that what this is, death? How long is he going to lay there?* As the minutes ticked by the finality of what he just did was becoming apparent to him. The magnitude of his actions rendered him in a state of prolonger paralysis as the suffocating thoughts continued rushing into his head like vultures descending upon a carcass.

Slowly he began to regain his senses. How long he stood there motionless was unknown but he noticed the progression of the sun's position as he began to think again. There were no more voices in his head telling him how to solve his new "problems." He remained standing above the body far too long, contemplating the subconscious thoughts that were surfacing in his mind. After an extended length of time he reached a point of lucidity where it all began to come clear to him. The sun continued to advance. Reality and the certainty of his action was cascading in with ever increasing speed. "This is murder," he said. Like large ocean waves crashing onto the rocky shore the thoughts of his prospective future were buffeting his emotions. These too was becoming too much for him to contain. He began to get nervous and to quake as he considered the fully anticipated reactions of family members once they knew. The thought of their eventual discovery was the primary idea that was dominating his comprehension. *They are going to want to kill me.* Again, Cain dropped down and tucked his head into his hands and between his knees. "Why did I do it, where can I run?" he asked himself. Still no more voices to give him any continued "useful suggestions."

He looked up as he remained crouched down beside his fallen brother to contemplate as many of the factors that he could consider before making his next move. "Abel, Cain spoke, you were a very loved and special person. You always respected our parents and honored them in every interaction you had with them. Ever since your boyhood days you knew the value of treating all family members as precious, even me. How could anybody not love you? All of our siblings felt close to you. You made them feel valued, as if their concerns truly were important to you," Cain spoke these words to his dead brother while weeping.

Will they wonder where he is? After all, he is a grown man and shouldn't need a keeper. How long will it be until they start missing him? Will they ask me questions about his whereabouts? Cain's imaginings were beginning to take on even more added weight in his mind and he was beginning to get frantic.

He continued talking to Abel, "Come on Abel, Abel, wake up." There was no response. He began to shake his brother's body but it felt as if it was getting cold to touch. He shook harder, not really knowing what else to do. Cain then grabbed his brother's shoulders and sat him up. His fleshy face was beginning to take on a grayish hue. Cain let out a startled yelp, "what is that?" he said. This was the first time in history a man looked into the eyes of a body whose life has gone out of it. Abel's eyes were fogging over. The strange, encroaching effects that death had upon Abel's body were unnerving to Cain. He now understood the finality of his action and that Abel will not be coming back, *he is gone forever.* That thought hit him with a thud.

Ominous!

He began to shake harder as he remained there. Cain put his head in both hands again as he called out to God, this time desiring His help. "What did I do? How can I go on from this?" There was no reply to his prayer. "I killed him, I murdered my own brother," he said aloud.

He realized that he did not want his family to connect him to the death of the beloved Abel.

I can't let them catch me, he thought. *The best thing to do is to move him and hide his body, I better drag it off and away from the altar. People looking for Abel would certainly look here, his mind kept racing. My father will look around the altar first. If he doesn't find him here he will probably expand his search to the field where Abel was working.*

Abel's body was getting difficult to move. "Jeez, I had no idea he was so heavy," Cain said to himself. To add to his difficulties the body didn't fold like it used to. Cain couldn't even get the arms to bend at the elbows, they were stiff like young branches, "what the heck"? Every time he got one arm to fold across Abel's chest it quickly straightened out and fell to his side again.

He then tried grabbing his brother by the ankles and pulling, dragging him feet first. That approach met with greater success, but the back of the victim's head was scraping the ground. After noticing a trail behind Abel's head Cain stopped tugging at the ankles, "this method did nothing for the open wound," he mumbled. There was an obvious trail of mixed soil and blood forming in the drag marks behind his head. Cain noticed the marks in the ground. He realized it would lead any search party straight to the stashed body. In order to eliminate this problem he ripped a low hanging leafy branch off of a nearby tree and swept the trail left to right starting at the altar and leading all the way into the woods. "That should do the trick unless, of course, they bring some of the dogs to scent him out," Cain mumbled again as he rubbed his hands together to clean them off.

Once the body was safely concealed inside the cover of the tree line, Cain quickly went back to his own work area where his altar was. There was still a smoldering wisp of smoke rising up from the remaining grain offering. He didn't have a shovel in his supplies there but found a spade with which he hurriedly ran back to the burial site. Upon arriving back at the body, he felt secure that the blood path from Abel's head would remain undetected. "It looks good to me but there is no telling what will happen if they bring the hounds, I must continue working to prevent that." was his one concerning thought.

He began to dig as the sun was setting. Judging by its angle in the sky, he estimated, that he had an hour and a half to carve out a shallow grave, drag some rocks from Abel's altar into the woods, stash and cover the body, and then return to the house without raising too much suspicion. *I have to work fast though.*

As he did, he began to feel a growing sense of control over the situation. While he dug the long but shallow hole and retrieved the rocks he began to consider his story, an alibi.

Another quick look at the sun and Cain knew from its location that he had to work with an even more deliberate pace. There was so much manual effort to do in order to save his own life. The story and more importantly, the scene, had to hide all evidence that pointed back at him. "With time running out I think I better focus on a rock solid story. There is not enough daylight left to remove all evidence of foul play. If my story is convincing the murder site won't even be a factor, no one will even think to come and look for him here," Cain said congratulating himself.

"*Abel was working his livestock and tending the sheep in the southwest sector of the estate. I was working my crops in the north,*" his lie began. "We *were supposed to meet up during our break for the evening atonement sacrifice, just like we promised, but Abel never showed up,*" according to his story. Cain then decided to include that *he needed to perform his religious duty alone, not knowing the whereabouts of his coworker, the lie continued.* This would have the effect of making him look righteous. *After all I had to keep my obligation and Abel is responsible for himself.* "*Once I completed my devotions I went back to work in the field. At that time I had no idea what became of Abel. So I decided to check on him before returning home. When I arrived in the southwest sector all I saw was a hastily erected altar with the remains of a sacrificed lamb on it. I yelled his name repeatedly, Abel, where are you?*" This was Cain's story.

The sun was no longer in the sky and it was dark outside before he arrived home. Cain was perspiring profusely as he walked in the door. People in his family noticed that and thought it odd. "Why are you so late? Why are you so sweaty? Where is your brother?" came the questions from his older sister. Upon over hearing this talk from the adjacent room Adam stepped in to the conversation. Cain looked at his father and continued to perspire, now from anxiety. He explained how he fell behind schedule because he was looking so long for Abel, "so I had to run home, he explained. I didn't want to be out in the wild after dark with dangerous animals all around searching for an easy kill." He replayed his alibi just like he rehearsed it before and during his jog home. No one seemed to suspect anything unusual. Cain thought, *I just might get away with it*. He added, "I just figured that Abel must have finished his work early and returned home without me after his sacrifice."

Adam sensed that something was amiss. He listened as Cain went on about his evening in the field and how he didn't know where Abel could be. An awful and dreadful feeling was growing inside him. Adam experienced this before, at the tree, in the garden. A sinking sensation like all the water draining through a hole in the bottom of a bucket overcame him. He felt woozy and said, "I need to sit down."

After regaining the strength to continue he said, "Where is Abel? He did not return home at his customary time." Adam's condition continued to get worse. A powerful nausea was controlling him now. His protective instincts for Abel were escalating, he was very worried. His daughters went to their father to comfort him.

"How does he know that something awful happened?" The younger daughter asked. "Maybe there is a simple explanation and this will all clear up as soon as Abel walks through the door," the sister replied.

For the first time since day six of the creation week, the sun could not come up fast enough. The hours just crawled by and Adam stared at the moon while sitting outside waiting, hoping for Abel to finally arrive. He strained his eyes peering into the darkness in the direction that he expected his son to return from. The staring did nothing to relieve his anxiety, he was realizing. Occasionally Adam dozed off into a fitful slumber only to be accosted by a short nightmare before sputtering awake again. After each dream episode Adam felt increasingly sure of the doom of his beloved son and where he was going to begin his search once the dawn broke. In the meantime he was going to continue to wait on and call out to God, his old Friend from those beautiful times before they ever encountered that serpent. "Oh, if I could only get Your attention the way I used to when we laughed and talked and worked and played together," Adam prayed.

"Where is he? Just tell me where he is. Please, God, come down here like the old days and walk with me as in times past. I need you! I can't make it without my son. Help him, protect him, bring him home safe so we can be a family together again. I'm sorry for what wrong things I have done and mostly for rejecting You and eating the fruit from that tree. That damned old tree, he cursed. I told You that I wouldn't and yet, I did partake of it. I saw how utterly disappointed you were in me and how I broke Your heart. As You turned and walked away from us for the last time and didn't look back I realized that I let my best Friend down. That was what upset me most about what I did, please forgive me," he wept.

If Adam was expecting or just hoping that God would arrive or bring Abel home at that very moment in response to that prayer, it did not happen. "How could I have been so stupid? He continued to blame himself, I ruined everything, and now this. Please, God, don't let anything bad happen to Abel and bring him home to me now." Adam would soon find out that his efforts were too late but that God would bring justice for the crime committed.

God was very dismayed by what happened to Abel. He too

loved the boy and tried to restrain Cain and Satan from killing him. God knew, however, what Adam had yet to realize. "Sin brings death to all! Both the guilty like Adam and Cain will die because of it, but all Adam's descendants cannot get out of deaths way in time because of it. Therefore, sin is loose in the creation because of the rebellion at the tree and it will rack up an impressive streak of victories over all the offspring of Adam and Eve until the day that the Seed comes and crushes the serpents head. In that glorious day life will reign once again," God rejoiced. "Adam has yet to discover that Abel is not the Seed but is one who needs Him," Adam could not hear Jehovah's reply.

Everyone in the family was up very early the next morning, way earlier than their usual time. Adam made sure that no time was wasted eating breakfast. "There was no time to lose. Abel might still be out there in need of our help," he told them. He instructed his younger son to go get some of the dogs to help with the search. "Get the tracking dogs, he told him and put them all on a leash," he said. Even Cain was up with them, acting worried and eager to help. When he heard his father command for the dogs Cain's strength wilted. *I hope they follow my story and search for him in the south, or I am doomed.* He was worried but not that Abel would speak to them of what happened. *If they find him at all, they will have to figure it all out without any real knowledge from me*, he thought. He then fell into the search party with the younger brother, the dogs and all of his other brothers, sisters and kinfolk to begin the search.

"Abel, "Abel," where are you? Everybody in the party called out. They soon spread out to cover more distance but all the bands walked in the same direction. They all kept calling out his name and anything else that they thought might aid in their search. Sometimes Adam would yell, "Silence!" to the searching groups in order to listen for any possible response from Abel. He would cup his hands behind his ears and strain to hear a sound. "Just one sound, any sound from him, one more sound, God, come on, let me hear it," he cried. But no sound from Abel ever came back. The groups all continued walking toward the place that Adam suspected they might find him, in the direction of the northwest sector. Cain was aghast. *How did he know to go there? I told him the south not the north,* He thought. *Maybe God did give him some sort of answer,* Cain mused. *They might find him,* he thought. *If they do what will I do then?*

The dogs were pulling hard on their tethers. The poor little brother inadvertently grabbed the lead of one of the larger canines, so when the dogs' blood began to run the brother struggled to maintain the animal. Soon all of the dogs picked up Abel's scent and the big one pulled the youngster off of his feet in excitement. He dragged the boy forward for a good 20 yards. Those in his team stepped in to stop him from being dragged any further by corralling the big beast. Adam told his sons to switch dogs. His young son handed the large dog to his brother who in return gave him one much smaller. "This one should be better suited for you little fella, his older brother said, we don't need to be about looking for you both in the same day." Once the lad was securely behind his new search partner that he was able to control, they all let the trackers lead them on their way. Finally one of the daughters yelled, "What is that over there? Everyone looked to see an altar with thin wisps of smoke still rising upward from the embers of the wood and the remains of the sacrificial lamb. All the searchers elongated they're strides and so covered ground much more quickly. As they arrived there at the scene, Adam and Eve broke down and began to sob. "That is his little lamb that he left the house with, cried Eve, Abel was here, something has happened to him." Once again Cain felt like he was getting closer and closer to being found out, he resented his father for not

9

believing him and taking the search parties north instead of south.

Everyone knew Abel had to be in the area. "Did a hungry predator get him and tear him to pieces as he sacrificed?" Came one suggestion. "Maybe the smell of the burning animal attracted a carnivore to their son," a sibling said. "We have got to find him, spread out again and go into the forest," came the order from Adam. Cain was once again beginning to sweat, "it's from all this searching activity," he said as he was getting angry that the party neared completion of their search. He knew he had one last chance to try to hide it. As the different groups pushed their way into the foliage the observant sisters yelled, "Look over here." Everybody ran to the location that she was directing them to. They couldn't see him, but Satan was there too, still admiring his work.

CHAPTER TWO

Everyone approached the mound of dirt and stones that were just ahead. Upon arriving they all stood there motionless and stared at a long pile of hand selected rocks which seemed to have been placed there by design. A large colorful snake was coiled up on the rocks. "Stand back, one of the daughters yelled, go get a big stick to smash that ugly thing to death," she yelled to anyone. The serpent just looked at them, coiled to strike with his tongue darting in and out before finally slithering away into the brush. "It sure looks like someone put all these rocks here. It looks like something is buried under them, said a searcher.

"Oh my God! Is that Abel?" Cried Eve.

All of the separate search groups formed one party at the pile of stones. They hoped against hope that the scene did not conceal what they feared most. By now the thought that the "worst" might have actually happened to Abel pervaded the thoughts of each family member although none said those words.

"Is, is, is thaaatt Abel under those rrrockkks?" The oldest sister finally asked. A shrill scream rose from the lips of her mother as the first stone was pulled away. At that moment most of Abel's face was now uncovered and his eyes, still open, seemed to be staring right at Eve. *Was he saying something to her?* She sure thought he was. As if speaking from the dead, "how could you have taken the fruit from that serpent and eaten it"? Eve fell down in a clump at the foot of the grave.

"If only I had believed God and you, Adam, and listened to

your words instead of the lies. If I had obeyed His command at that time rather than doing what I wanted to do," Eve whimpered. She felt his death should be laid at her feet. "If not for my foolish decisions at the temptation nobody would have to face this." She broke down into a deep and guttural wail of agony.

"Oh God, that's my baby, my precious son, my son. We had hope that he was the one who would crush the serpents head. Now he's dead," she said inconsolably. Gradually everyone pulled themselves away from her and began to collect themselves. They started piecing bits of information together. "It wasn't an animal that did this, he was not tore to pieces." "How else could the stones have been so neatly placed on top of him except by a person? It had to be a human," the conversations continued. Instantly Cain interjected: "let's not jump to any conclusions here. Let's be sure of what happened before we start placing blame. Maybe he was attacked or did it to himself." At that comment every single person's icy stare snapped right to Cain with ever growing suspicion. Cain was sounding and beginning to look very ridiculous. *Did he just say that?* "He is the guilty one," they all yelled. In mass their hostility grew as the group grabbed at Cain. "Hold him fast, don't let him go for justice must be served," growled a brother.

Adam was furious too. Eve was beyond being comforted. "How could he have done that to him?" They asked each other. Most of Abel's siblings wanted to punish Cain most severely right then and there. "He deserves to die," some said. They spoke openly about different ways to kill him as the justice for murdering a better, more righteous man.

Cain was not able to get away from his would be executioners.

Afterward they escorted him to the family estate. His hands and feet were tied together with the leather cords that were the dog leashes. At the estate he was then secured to a post that was planted deep into the ground. After many days of questioning him and putting forth ideas of how they think he might have done it, Cain began to soften.

Members of the family went back and forth to the crime scene to study the clues, bury Abel and try to figure out just how and why Cain killed his brother. *It seems to have happened in the field in front of Abel's altar and during his sacrifice. It looks like there was a trail from there to the edge of the forest.* The prisoner continued to hold out but realized that his captors were not going to kill him. He knew he would have to confess to it all soon. The Lord had assured him that "no man will slay me without receiving vengeance from God seven fold." He put a sign on Cain as a token that he had been given his sentence and justice had been decreed to unfold in him throughout the rest of his life. The death penalty, however justified, was not permitted in this case. Cain began to take his confidence from that conversation they had in the field, with God.

God is merciful after all, thought Cain.

Finally he came to where he wanted to explain everything to Adam and Eve just as it happened, how it occurred and why he did it. He told them that "he will confess in the morning, I want my younger brother to be there too as a condition," he said.

Everyone in the family was satisfied that Cain was finally going to tell the truth, "but why did he include such a strange condition? The elder brother asked. Be careful father, he cautioned Adam, don't untie his hands with the youngster so close to him," he demanded.

"We will make sure we take all necessary precautions before we do this, he answered, but we must find out from Cain's own lips what happened."

The next morning the prisoner began confessing and he spared no detail. His story began, "after working for our usual number of many long hours in the field, Abel with the animals and me with the crops, we took our extended break. We planned on sacrificing together at a common alter but personalities being what they were, we then decided it would be better to offer our sacrifices separately. Abel was really getting on my nerves all day long about his atonement. He was so excited, singing, discussing plans and even naming his sacrificial lamb. Abel kept saying it was the perfect offering, spotless and without blemish. Why did he have to keep boasting in his little lamb? He just wouldn't shut up about it. I did not feel, at all, the same way about my offering as he did about his. My plan was to sacrifice the best wheat and corn that I had picked from the field. He kept telling me: 'no, no, brother that will never do! This is a sacrifice of atonement to wash away our sins with the blood of the innocent. Crops will never gain God's acceptance'", he said.

"Enough! I answered-. You think God only likes you but I got news for you brother, He will accept my sacrifice and me too." Cain became visibly agitated just in the retelling of their dialogue. He was visibly angered in the recounting about Abel's actions and not at all over any of his own. "I told him to take his lamb and his evangelical zeal and make his offering somewhere far from me. 'Of course, brother, if you think that is best,' is all he said before leaving."

Cain paused before continuing, "I made an altar with rocks from the field. I piled on the wood and lit the fire. Off in the distance I could hear Abel, again being annoying, praying and worshipping so loudly. As my fire grew hotter I put more and more crops on it until a still small voice spoke to me in my soul. I knew the God I worked so hard to please was not looking at me with favor due to my effort. Just as a fire burned on the altar so also a fire of anger burned in me. I became incensed and felt intense hatred as the heat welled up in my face. Cain was visibly red faced and angry again. He continued, although I couldn't see it, my face felt as if it got all hard and twisted. My mouth and forehead felt extremely contorted into strange defects and as long as I thought of Abel, it only got worse.

That voice spoke to me again and said, "Why is your face looking like that? Do the righteous thing then you and you're offering will be accepted by Me. As it is now, sin is at the door, pressing in to control you, don't let that happen."

I yelled at the still small voice and said, "Quiet down!" It felt as if I was going crazy and I put my head between my knees as I fell to the ground. I couldn't think of anything to help the situation and I was unable to get up. I have never been that angry before. Then another thought came into my mind like a stampede of cattle, 'you can silence him, go over there and make him be quiet." After what seemed like forever, I finally regained my feet and headed over to Abel's altar to see him. *It was time to put a stop to all of his shenanigans and get to finishing up on our labors for the day*, I thought.

Abel was facing towards his altar as I approached him he did not really seem concerned at my coming. I noted that *his altar obviously was not nearly as impressive as mine.* There were some places in his structure that he never even filled in with stones. I mean, that was so ridiculous and he kept saying how right **he** was. He was more interested in the animal and performing his obligation than having everything look just right. As I got near I found a rock that I thought would fit perfectly on the top row where there was an obvious hole, so I picked it up intending to make an improvement upon his shoddy work.

I commanded him that he meet me as I walked out toward the field. It was imperative that we transition back to our labors. He looked at me and took two steps toward his sacrifice on the altar and began worshipping-again. Ugh! He didn't even listen to me or care anything about what I just said. The next thing that happened, I can't explain why but I ran up to him from behind and hit him on the back of the head with the rock that was still in hand. I did that too hard, much harder than I intended. It did not occur to me that the rock would supply much greater force than if I had hit him without one. I only wanted to shake him up and to get him back to what was important, **Cain lied**. He fell motionless at my feet and as I looked at him I panicked. His face did not look good. Then I saw his blood leaking out from the back of his head and getting all over the base of the altar. There was so much blood that it mingled in with the blood of the lamb. Then there was an awful groaning sound rising up from the ground beneath us and I thought, when I first heard it, that it was him. From somewhere behind me came another sound of heinous laughter and then I knew the groaning sound wasn't coming from Abel at all." Adam and Eve shook violently upon hearing Cain describe the groaning sound.

"*Was somebody watching? Had they seen the whole episode? Who did that laughing?* Immediately I started planning on how best to conceal his body, so I dragged him into the trees in order to stash him and then I covered up his body with rocks."

Cain then broke from his confession and turned to face his angriest family members, "I know that some of you want to kill me but beware, he told them, God said that you will receive seven times worse punishment than I am going to get if you do that. God spoke audibly to me while I was in the field coming from the woods."

"Where is Abel?" God asked.

"I don't know,' I said, 'am I my brother's keeper?" I snarked.

"That eerie groaning sound that you heard was Abel's blood, it was crying out to the One he worshipped," God said.

Cain continued the revelation as if he was in a trance, reliving the conversation he had with God. "Now the Righteous One will begin executing His judgment upon me. You must allow me to go immediately, now that I have told you, so that you do not get entangled in the sentence I must serve. Who knows that the Righteous One will not bring destruction to all if you prevent me from serving His term of justice? The longer you keep me here makes it harder for those who want to kill me to restrain themselves from doing so. For their own sake, release me before they can no longer prevail over their lust for vengeance."

Cain continued, "God has sentenced me to wander the earth as a vagabond and to scratch out a living away from the soil. No longer will the ground produce anything for me, I must learn a new way to survive. Gone are the glorious days with you all around me and our sumptuous feasts during meals. God has marked me and now I am destined to roam with no man willing to help me. I am cut off from the land of the living, my sin and failure to gain mastery over it has done me in. But I can assure you that Abel is in a better place. He is with the Maker and he was smiling even in death."

At the sound of those words, Adam and Eve dropped to the ground. Both of them were sobbing uncontrollably about what once was, dreams now lost and what it now is. "This is a loss that I shall never recover from," said Eve.

Their children went to them and comforted each one, but having been alive from the very beginning, they both knew too much. Every event that occurred from then until now is recorded in their minds and they remember everything. Their memories were replaying the scenes that, through the decades, have led up to this precipitous set of events. "How can we pick up and continue on, knowing everything that we did and did not do?" Eve stammered. It was all becoming clear as crystal. The cause and effect dynamics that gradually escalated into the murder of their beloved son at the hands of his brother. It could all be laid at their feet and they understood that bitterly. This was a wound for them that would never go away until they also died, as God said they would. Never before has that truth been so understandable. Cain continued to suggest that it would be best for the entire family if he was released and sent on his way at once. He spoke, "just by me being here, having done what I did, is not helpful to anybody. I should move on and begin my new life as a wanderer as God has decreed. He continued his discourse, it's not like I would be the first and only one who ever left the family estate to begin a new life on his own."

Through the decades Adam and Eve have been very faithful to the command to be fruitful and multiply. Their only family planning consisted of having as many children as the Lord gave them. They knew that their obedience gave the assurance of God's provision. They have raised dozens and dozens of children and many of them have grown up and moved away to begin their own legacy.

Cain suggested again that they consent to allow him to follow through on God's order, so all will be well for the rest of them. "I have done enough damage to you, and don't wish to be responsible for any more," he said.

The angriest siblings were the first to speak and the consensus was that Cain was right. Increasingly more voices consented with the larger opinion that saying goodbye to Cain immediately and forever is the right and best thing to do for everybody. Finally, the parents relented and began the process toward separating with another son. "Death and separation feel the same to me, said Adam. They both are like twin fawns of the same doe." "That's how it works, we are separated from God and some day to die. Abel died which brings about this separation from Cain," replied a tearful Eve. The terms of their coming estrangement where nothing like what any of them imagined through Cain's formative years. "He had so much promise, his mother said, and so much potential. He was a good boy, faithful to the family and devoted to making it stronger. But sin played its ugly hand in his life and ruined everything." In their hearts both of them understood and withheld resentment from Cain. They also failed cataclysmically when sin approached them personally, and they both painfully remember that all too well. Their fault, in time, led to this result, they reasoned. But oh, they never realized then just how devastating sin would become or how painful death would feel, especially to the survivors.

The next morning came and they were sending him off. A single pack mule was loaded with as much food, supplies and sustenance as it could carry. Cain was given some currency for emergency situations. "After all, hadn't he worked so hard through his decades of productivity? he deserved it," Adam said. "Didn't he really make everybody's life better with the produce of his labors? He deserved the best possible start that we can provide him," agreed Eve. Many of his siblings refused to even acknowledge him that morning. They did not see things as their parents did in helping Cain out with his departure. Good riddance and never come back was their only sentiment. Finally, their brother departed and wound up going toward the east. The parents watched him go until he disappeared with his mule into the horizon.

CHAPTER THREE

I t took a couple days for things on the estate to begin to resemble normalcy again. Adam was very conscientious about comforting his wife. She was still very beautiful and in his eyes has only gained in appearance through their long time together. *She has always been a good help mate and companion.* Eve never complained about her responsibilities but always was faithful to them. She was and is a good mother. Adam understood how much she means to him and so he was very consoling to her. She appreciated his efforts and did take comfort in his love and embrace. Finally they were intimate again and she conceived another child. In nine months the newborn would arrive. There was great apprehension in their hearts about the prospects, however. Would he grow up to be like Cain or Abel?

The heavenly Father never actually left the presence of His beloved creation. Although Adam and Eve never experienced the same level of closeness with Him after their fall He was always with the family members in revealing Himself to each one. Their sin had made a wall between them but the Lord was determined to tear it down. He loved Adam, Eve and all of their children and continued working in their lives through daily events toward the implementation of His plan. "My ultimate objective is and always has been to eliminate the dividing wall of sin and uniting each person to Myself," He said. He is unable to overlook the facts of people being mired in the sinful state of rebellion that they are in and Himself being all together righteous. This brought about an unworkable contrast where the sinner could not abide with Him. If the Father would ignore their condition and force Himself into their fellowship the result would be catastrophic. His righteousness would blaze and by the force of its own nature He would annihilate the sin and drive it far from Him. The human, as a result, would get caught up in the inferno and end up in total destruction. "No, not that", God said. His plan was wonderful and when, in the fullness of time it is revealed, it will show His love and righteous judgment together all at the same time.

"Let His mercy and justice tumble down like water over a hill. Sacrifice is the cost and life will be the outcome so that death will be swallowed up in victory," The Word rejoiced. It is a mystery known only in the mind of God, but He longs for it to be revealed to those He loves and it is ever unfolding.

"Should we name him Abel?" The question came up but it didn't last long before being dismissed. "We cannot name him Abel." They agreed. Adam and Eve continued the discussion of a proper name for the newborn boy. In the continuance of their recovery from their painful loss Eve bore her soul to her husband. "I know that I am ultimately responsible for all that has gone wrong in this world. I should have run when that deceiver opened our dialogue. Instead, I entertained his destructive ideas and listened to him turn it all around so that it looked like his offer was something wonderful. If I had just stayed true to the Word of the Lord and told the deceiver what God said instead of what I thought, then we wouldn't all be in this condition at this time," she said.

"Now we both are paying for it. First, I hurt you and now we lost our precious boy. But God is merciful and comforts us in our affliction. He has compensated us for our loss with this baby. Let's name him **Seth**, for he is appointed by God to replace Abel." Adam laughed in delight. "The mother of all flesh is finding new life in this new special little newborn blessing," he said.

"Yes I do exalt in God my savior, but I so long for the coming of the Seed. Now that we have tasted death and felt the grip of its icy grasp I am seeing wickedness increase. It is like my eyes are opened now even more than when we were in the Garden," she said.

"I am experiencing the same thing, my love, he replied. Perhaps Seth is the one we are all looking to be the One, the Seed." he said.

The sting of sin was beginning to inflict a continuous but low level of pain at all times upon the world's population. The curse of rebellion that began in Adam and Eve has been passed down to all their children. There was not one person on earth that was not infected with it. As sinners they were becoming more and more degraded in their behavior and debased in their mind.

Adam and his wife often commented to each other "how much the people were getting worse. The things they do these days were unheard of in the old days," she said. At times something more severe, such as another reported murder, would be done and their pain level would spike upward. In time, however, the discomfort over the hearing of it would drop back down to a more tolerable plateau. As the years continued to pass though, they noticed that the threshold was generally higher than it used to be in the beginning. "People used to be ashamed to be seen doing some of the things that are being done out in the open these days, She told him. Sinful behavior is more and more frequent, people are so brazen about it and it is increasingly severe. Sin seems to be alive and have a growing life of its own as an irresistible force," she finished. Some of Adam and Eve's grown children were so controlled by their sin infection that they no longer even resembled what their parents remembered them to be and they no longer knew them. "When will the One who is to be the Seed of the woman come and stomp out this devil's disease? We have waited for so long to see Him," they mourned.

The parents couldn't wait for Seth to grow up and reach the age of manhood. "He is a special boy, but will he continue to seek and call on God when he is a man?" As it was, they could see something that was different about Seth that was similar to how Abel was. Seth loved God and sought for Him. He often said that he "wanted others to seek Him too."

He was a good-looking young man that, before long, grew up to be tall and strong. Many of the adults in the community sought him out for important jobs when they had to have a reliable hand. Seth was someone who understood the importance of earning trust through consistent effort and performance and he earned a good reputation with everyone in his hometown. He was known for giving an honest day's work for a day's wage. He often said to his friends, "you will never prosper without the favor of God and man. I would rather win favor in the eyes of my neighbors than cheat them for a short term gain. Once they respect you, then comes influence." Seth never went a day without being gainfully employed and in high demand.

As he aged into manhood many of the local girls noticed his beauty and competed with each other for his attention. Some of the girl's fathers even tried to make a deal with him so that they could give their daughter's hand to him in marriage. One father offered him "a position as partner in my cattle business if you will take my daughter to be your wife." Another father who heard about that offer quickly countered and told Seth, "I will make you a 10% partner in my silver mine if you will marry my daughter." Regardless of these and many other offers, no one could get him to accept any of their propositions.

Seth knew what he was looking for, however, and *was saving himself for that right woman.* He considered his own mother to *be his example of a good wife and woman.* Most importantly he understood and often said, "a woman that fears the Lord was above prize." Once the local girls realized that he felt that way, more than a few tried the straight and narrow approach in order to win his heart. Other suitors considered that method to be too long of a shot for them. "I would never be able to convince him that I have pious virtues, Seth would certainly see right through my charade and reject me outright," said one. "The same is true for me, sister, I have never been into religion so that trick wouldn't work for me either, but I sure am into Seth," her companion giggled. These girls of lesser interest in spiritual matters tried the sensual approach by tempting him with their flesh. "I can't believe he turned down my very sensuous offer," said a third girl. Regardless of their method, Seth was no easy catch. He simply repeated, "I am not going to compromise on the one decision that is considered to be the most important one I can make in order to be successful," he said.

In time, Adam and Eve stopped having babies. They did not plan on that happening, they simply conceived no more children. Adam was 130 years old when he begat Seth and many were born after him. They thought Seth must be the Seed who was to come. "Who else could it be?" He and Eve said.

The man and his wife had dominion over the earth and its creatures but they could do nothing about the advance of time.

The steady march of the days into weeks, into months and then into years resulted in everybody getting older. Adam and Eve never knew what it was like to be very young. Being a baby, a child, an adolescent, were never in their Maker's plan for them. They were always adults and now the only ones left and alone in their large house with all of their kids moved out. By the time the last of their children left and was living elsewhere most of Adam and Eve's older children were having babies and grandchildren of their own. "Be fruitful..... Fill the earth." God said.

Everyone knew that Seth was eager to start a family of his too, however, but only through the right way. "Since my young adulthood I have been preparing for the challenges of marriage and fatherhood. In my estimation, selecting the right woman to marry is secondary in importance to being the right man in that marriage. I have watched and seen other families and noticed that the success to failure ratio rested squarely on the husband. If the man was devoted to his wife and children and strong in his leadership and discipline, but compassionate and patient toward the needs of his family, then a happy and successful family was the result. For the ones that love their wife and would sacrifice themselves for her as well as instruct the children daily in the way that they should go, a legacy of influence and prosperity always followed," he instructed. Many of his peers did not understand this to be true, but Seth sure did. His friends often ridiculed him for being so straight, "Seth, how can you pass up on that girl's offer? She wants to give it all to you tonight and she is so good looking," they would say. His friends enjoyed being with him because he was a good friend to them but especially because they got close to the best looking young women that would work very hard just to get next to Seth. "Maybe Seth can hook me up with one of his cast offs," was their common reply.

Finally Seth did meet the woman of his and God's choosing.

She was what he was always looking for. Adam and Eve were also thrilled with this prospect for their beloved son. Her parents also could not have been more pleased. Her father did not have much money or power "but he did a great job raising a good woman," Seth delighted.

They married at a relatively young age. Both he and she wanted to have children. She believed "this was one of the main purposes of a family," she often said. Sons and daughters were later begotten of them and each one was very precious to both. He instructed each child of the essential truth that God created all that is seen and unseen from that which is unseen. "He simply spoke the Word and gave the commandment and it then came into being. Everything was made from that which was not because He created it with His Word. Do you understand that?" he asked. It never ceased to amaze him that little children understood and believed the truth with no reservations at all. He told them "to seek God and to call upon His name. You need Him for redemption of your soul because all people are sinful and have fallen short of His righteous requirements. "They might all live for a very long time but it is appointed unto them that they eventually will die and face the judgment," he said to his wife. Seth so wanted all of his children to live their lives as preparation for the certainty of that event and the life thereafter. Due to his gentle, consistent and persevering ways, his children all adhered to his instruction and followed his example in their own lives.

At times Seth departed from the family for a couple weeks at a time to journey through his "preaching circuit." A well warn and constructed path that went from stop to stop where he would deliver his sermons to the faithful. He was quite a preacher and many of his childhood friends were not surprised by this at all. While he was away during one of his tours he began to write down many things in a book that he thought were important and related to his call and mission. Everything his father told him and that he had learned, continuing into present day, was recorded in the book. The only focus of events for his book were those things related to the coming Seed. *"The notes are rudimentary but I will put it all into much clearer thought at a later time,"* he told himself. In his writings he recorded the creation week, the making of his parents, the garden, the fruit, the serpent, the temptation and fall, the eviction, and how the family lines follow certain lineages. He discussed God and His prophecy of the coming Seed that will restore God's relationship with people and His creation, primarily. "This is a good start but this catalog of those events must be organized for the long term," he said after each entry.

When Seth was 105 years old he had another son and named him Enosh because the Lord had given him another son. The fire of Seth's hope had previously dimmed but it once again was lit as if a smoldering ember had reignited into an inferno. He had been growing weary, not in his joy in the God of his father, but by the ever encroaching wickedness of his fellow man. He knew from long discussions with Adam that the state and condition of man has only grown toward evil continually. "It seems like all my preaching, all of my travel and sacrifice, the toil of the travel, all of it has been for nothing," he confided in his father. "You have greatly beaten back the curse of thorns and now enjoy a bountiful harvest, Seth said to Adam, why can't I gain any ground on the curse that I am contending with through my ministry?" He asked. Years and years ago Adam explained the entire sin dynamic to him. He testified that "it is a disease that is always eating its way into and through the core of every human being. As it bores its way into the soul it leaves a trail of ruination in lives, communities, societies, and most critically, communion with the Maker." Seth asked as he was beginning to think "are we the only ones left. Everybody else had given themselves over to the evil within them. There was none that were good, no one sought after God," he mused. Then God, as if the answer to Seth's prayer, gave him a son, Enosh.

CHAPTER FOUR

Seth could easily grasp the history of the world. It was close to 300 years and running since the creation. "I can see the destruction that the path everybody is on is leading to," was the title of one of his sermons. "Turn from your wayward ways and embrace His saving hand," he cried out. On his circuit, Seth expounded on the attributes of God as a being Who is loving and gracious. "He is just and righteous. He created man to fellowship with Him but man chose evil rather than righteous fellowship with his Maker. As a result of his willful sin, man is cut off from the joy of eternal life and doomed to death and destruction. God is holding out His hand to reach every one and deliver them from a certain and destructive end," he consistently reminded them, during a well known sermon. Come to Him now, He waits for you to call on His name," he bellowed.

When his son, Enosh, was just a stripling he was only interested in always being with his father Seth. His dad was a hero to him and he found his greatest joy in the presence of his father. As it was in this case, Enosh was a thirsty sponge that absorbed everything his dad said and did. He was always in class being tutored by the mastery of a true man. In time, as he grew up, the son encapsulated all of his father's lessons into this one and essential element: seek Jehovah and call upon His name. "As He did in his father's life, so will He prevail in mine."

He told his father, Seth, of this epiphany which he had and God blessed him even more than before because of it.

After he came of age Enosh finally got to join his father in running the preaching circuit. This was his only professional desire and like in everything else that he did, he came to embody his father's spiritual teachings.

Since his family had all grown up the circuit became a much more frequently travelled path than in the past. Seth had always been a great and dynamic orator. Having grown up under the arms of Adam and Eve, he eagerly and often sought their counsel. This gift was given to him and so he had a most amazing perspective and insight concerning all things related to his flock.

Until that time no one ever gave much thought to Seth's message beyond the enjoyment of his skillful and passionate presentation. "Oh how he can put on a really big show" a fan would proclaim. While he was preaching Seth would always use every square inch of his platform and thus he would end up covered with sweat. His energy level was immense with his arms waving, fingers pointing, face expressing, and body jumping as he preached. "I have not enjoyed the harvest that I worked for and believed would surely have been mine by now, I eagerly wait for His answer," he said. Seth's emotional tank was running out of oil.

This all changed in the fullness of time after Enosh joined his father. The two formed quite a dynamic duo. They were quite possibly the first tandem that worked together on earth for a greater purpose than their own self interests. Bringing in the harvest simply meant, "more souls in the kingdom of God which is good for anyone," Seth commented. On most nights the two preachers would ascend the platform to the pulpit and light the crowd ablaze with their fiery rhetoric and discourse. The men, women, and even children from all around would come from far away and nearby to listen to the two burning coals that were plucked from a blazing inferno. The people in the crowd walked, rode on horseback, camel's humps, mule's backs and even in cattle carts in order to attend just one event. Some people jumped in donkey dollies, ran, and even got there on piggy back" to see the show," as they called it. One man even got some friends to carry him on his stretcher all the way there. In time, all that heard came to believe and they also began to call on the name of the Lord. The circuit was becoming such a spectacle, like a ring of blazing fire, that it attracted unwanted attention as well.

Not everybody who came to the crowds was happy when the two preachers came to town. Some of the most wicked demons in Satan's army of bedraggled fallen ones also began attending the revivals in order to find out what all the community fuss was about. "Just what is all the hoopla that we keep hearing about these two preachers, and why does everybody get so animated about our Enemy when they are here?" asked Crepe.

They planned on reporting their findings to lord Satan on this "illegal activity" in hopes of gaining his favor and a promotion. The demonic spies would remain incognito as crowd members and often disguised themselves as the people who came up from out of the caves in order to seek the light. These "cave people" tended to be the lowest dregs of any community which had the misfortune of being inhabited by them. No one paid much if any attention to them. All the towns people have learned that the best thing to do regarding the "cave people" is ignore and avoid them. They were primitive and, generally, hunters of wolves and other large beasts. Every one of them smelled like something terrible all the time. Many discussions were made between the town's folk concerning the source in the mixture of the cave people's foul and pungent bodily odor. Some said it smelled like a combination of musk, their own urine and waste, as well as that of animal's waste, horrible body odor and moth balls. No one could bear their stench for long and would run out of their presence if they ever had the unhappy misfortune to collect a foul smelling waft in their nostrils. It was believed by all that the cave people liberally used moth balls to keep hungry predators out of their dwellings where they routinely leave scraps of uneaten food around their fire pits.

Over the decades of living in caves these subterranean brutes became prone to poor posture, hunched backs, stiff joints, unsocial manners, ignorant of all social graces and always the poorest among them. They were considered unintelligent beasts and for the most part, they were.

When Satan's two spies crept into the crowd during the meetings most of those in attendance quickly turned away from the "cave people" in order to avoid the predictable pungent stench. "Oh no, why did those nasty people have to come stand next to me? God, please don't let the wind blow this way" many in the crowd would say. Of course this reaction was anticipated by the demons, Crepe and Glutton, and it suited their cause to remain anonymous and undetected. After following the crowds for consecutive nights, the spies were confident that they knew exactly what to tell their leader. Crepe said to Glutton, "these two preachers are giving out strategy and combat orders to their new recruits, this is preparation for another war." Glutton replied, "We better not waste any more time now that we know what they are up to. You know how fast their King can strike once He is ready to do so." They had been firsthand witnesses of this and have now seen how the two firebrands would whip their assembly into an excited mass of humanity. "They lead all the people into praise of the hated One. All praise and honor to Jehovah's name, let His enemies be scattered," Glutton yelled to Crepe unable to bear the worship. The infiltrators had to cover their ears and scream to drown out the "noise." The ones standing next to them considered their actions to be a bit strange but "considering that they are cave people, what else should we expect?" they shrugged. The great God was also in attendance, with all this worship, and

He knew the enemy was there too. He was doing a great work.

Crepe and Glutton finally left the assembly to report their findings to Satan. "Come on Crepe, let's get out of here, we got to get back," said Glutton. "Hold your horses dude, I want to see how this show ends, I can't believe it's you telling me to hurry up" he replied.

"It's too late for you so we are leaving now without hearing another word," Glutton demanded.

Upon their arrival at their basecamp, as expected, the deceiver was wroth with anger upon hearing their news. "This other worldly intruder always has to try to sneak His nose under my tent flap, like a camel," Satan spewed. "Once again He is attempting to move in and expel us from our own rightful realm. I'll tell you what we are going to do, he continued, we will stomp his nose while it is still under the flap , before the rest of the camel follows its nose to get completely in," he said in analogy. "We will begin to pour out just what is required to dowse the flames of this little revival. After that, we will send out our own preachers to teach advanced lessons in the joy of doing evil. We will have our own revival."

An audience of miscreants began to assemble in mass when they heard that lord Satan was beginning one of his award winning rants. They all got there fast and chanted in approval as Satan spelled out the details. They yelled, "Bring on the fight, bring on the fight."

Satan was feeling it now and continued to jazz up the growing group. "All men will fall deeper than ever before thought possible and plunge headlong into the world of evil. "This is going to be great!" they replied.

There will never be another preacher capable of bringing them back. That Liar can hang His message on a tree for all to see and pound it in with a hammer and nails but it will all be for nothing. For every man will be so steeped in his own love for

CHRIS PAGANO

wickedness that God Himself won't even be able to turn them back. Even if He threatens them with a deluge of destruction for their obstinacy, what good will it do? They will be so enmeshed with their own schemes and sinfulness, their fate will be sealed from long ago," he finally finished his spatter.

Satan then looked out at his growing audience. He observed an uncountable mass of hideous treachery as all the demons were breaking out into manic celebration. They enjoyed his sermons so much they demanded for even more, an encore.

And so, seizing the opportunity before him, he continued. The devil began to glow with a bioluminescence, in pure anticipation of enacting his battle plan. Step by step he enumerated his strategy that would utilize deceptive doctrine, lies, lies, and more lies, all spoken in the form of news, gossip and the whisper. His favorite part of the plan, that he salivated over, was introducing the "sons of god" into humanity. The crowd got more excited but didn't understand what that meant. When he told Decapo about this part of his strategy, Decapo misunderstood and replied, "Why would you want sons of God to be used for anything?" Satan expected such a response and laughed in great delight. "Such an ingenious part of my plan that is so devious that no one can anticipate it and they certainly won't be able to thwart it," he said. Satan was going to unleash his newly conceived, secret and unstoppable weapon. "By using the sons of God I am going to spread my seed and forever change the very nature and DNA of the sons of Adam," he said.

"Who are they, asked Decapo, angels?"

"No, you sputtering jewel of ignorance, Satan reprimanded, not angels but ex-angels."

With all that being said, the plan was certified and ready to be put into action. "I will watch and wait for the right time to strike, you can all be sure that when that moment arrives, it will

34

happen," he told them. It's just a matter of time until the fires of revival begin to simmer down," he promised as he dismissed the frenzied throng. All the demons were never so ready to go out and wreak havoc upon the inhabitants of earth than they were as they were dismissed from the assembly.

With great patience the old serpent, again, went to work in anticipation for the hunt. He scouted out and got into perfect position and then waited for his opening. It took decades for an opportunity to be presented to him but eventually Seth and Enosh no longer travelled together as they aged.

News from home came to Seth and Enosh with a report that their mother and grandmother was sick and not expected to recover. Upon hearing of her condition they tried to get back to the estate in time but the news traveled to them so slowly that by the time they received it there wasn't much time left for her.

At home, Adam held his aged wife with her head on his lap as he encouraged her to turn her heart to their one true Friend. "He covered us with His sacrifice and you received it, my love," he told her. "You are going to be with Him soon. I will join you in His house when my time on earth is also finished."

She was ready to stop fighting and told her husband "I am weary of resisting and am ready to give in to the tug on my soul, His messengers beckon me." Shortly after, she passed on into the other world. The angels escorted her to their Father's presence where she was reunited with her son Abel, the Father, The Word, The Spirit and all those heavenly host. Adam was crushed by yet another blow from death. Again he felt the full weight of what he did all those hundreds of years ago. *Try not to think about it too deeply*, he thought.

A few days later Seth and Enosh arrived but it was obviously too late.

Satan had been very patient for the inferno of spiritual fervor to finally die down. As a result of his long suffering efforts he began to sense an opportunity. "Seth is old now, Enosh is not looking so eager for a fight anymore. There is definitely a cooling off in the spiritual atmosphere, he said, it won't be long now until I am going to introduce the plan and give them all hell," he whispered.

"Oh my God! What's that? Shrieked some of the town's folk as the huge human looking form lumbered down the middle of the street. It was not a human but it walked like a man, erect and on two legs. It brought the very presence of evil with it and the people in town could feel the conflict with sin arise in their own souls. Most of them still felt a connection to the spiritual life and the preachers so they could tell something bad was happening. The stranger had no intention of ever leaving and after a couple more days there was more of them. As the news of their arrival spread, reports came in from other towns of the same thing happening there as well. These beings came to live in every town where the preaching circuit had a podium. "What are they? And what are they doing here?"

Although the people of the town hoped and expected that the intruders would just pass on through their peaceful, happy lives and keep moving on their way to wherever it was that they were going, it turned out that their town, their lives, was that destination. The monsters were there to stay. Although the large new comers were ominous in appearance, their manner and conduct was congenial and respectful, at first. The giants were eager to gain the people's trust and continued to offer free labor to those who lived there. As a result, everybody slowly started to trust them and began to appreciate their help. "They're just big dumb friendly oafs," one man joked with his neighbor.

If anything needed to be moved or held up or stacked these large helpers were quite a "blessing." They were eager to assist their earthly hosts and even began seeking full time employment from their human friends in order to stay busy and to be able to buy what they needed. Little did the humans know this was all part of the scheme and everything was going according to Satan's perfect plan. Decapo gained a greater appreciation of his master having witnessed his patient perseverance resulting in apparent success. "These people are all suckers," he commented.

Eventually the local population of the sons of Adam began to get even more comfortable with their new oversized neighbors and routinely welcomed them into their social circles. The same people who once regularly attended the revival services even began bringing their daughters, as a result of these friendships, into contact with the "giants," as they were sometimes called.

Satan patiently watched as this dynamic unfolded. He summoned the leader of the giants, Anak, "Now that they trust you it is time to enact phase two of the plan and start moving in on their daughters. You must use the trust that you have gained to take as many wives as you desire from them and produce offspring according to our kind."

"It is plain to see that many of them are fair to behold and to be desired for that purpose, we will do as you wish lord Satan," Anak replied.

Everything was working exactly the way that lord Satan envisioned when he formed this strategy and the giants began fraternizing with the daughters of Eve. Social conditions were changing fast and the first one to arrive into town took a woman to be his wife. He said that "she pleases me and I desire her." Her father was a devotee of Seth and Enosh. He knew something was amiss and did not approve of his daughter's agreement to wed such an alien being. "I don't know if he is human, alien or something else entirely. But I do know he does not know the God we call on or serve Him in any way. There is an evil in him," the man said. The young newlywed wife tried to assure her father that there was nothing for him to worry about and insisted to him that she can influence her new husband and get him to change in order to serve their God.

The presence and activities of the sons of Anak began to split the townspeople's loyalties. At one point they turned the majority of the people to back them. Any of the other town's people that joined in protest did so to no avail. "After all, who was going to stop them anyway?" said a neighbor. Once the first union between a son of Anak and a daughter of Eve became final, many more other Rephaim and daughters of Eve joined in matrimony. Soon enough, more and more of the Rephaim that followed their leader into town also took a daughter of Eve to be their wife. All of the fathers that protested soon came to the full realization that there was nothing that they or anybody else could do about it. The giants were becoming only interested in doing as they pleased and not the least bit concerned or interested in how the fathers felt in response to their actions. They tried desperately to convince their daughters but they could never understand why their fathers wanted to keep true love from them. Each man, on the other hand, never understood how anyone could be so captivated by such an inhuman alien.

The giants were growing in boldness and becoming more aggressive in their dealings with the daughters of Eve. They were only interested in doing as they pleased and were not the least bit interested in how the girl's father felt about it.

Reph was overheard confessing to Anak, "we don't really even much care about actually getting married. To us marriage is nothing but a necessary step to get our own nose under the tent and gain some semblance of acceptance. "Until that time comes, when we can disregard that formality altogether, we must continue using this approach," demanded lord Satan to Anak. "Many of the most radical giants, in fact, took more than one of the daughters to betroth and other times just copulated with other young women for their own pleasure," retorted Reph. Upon hearing of this slight deviation from the plan Satan mumbled, "Genius." The man that was overhearing all of this ran off to tell Seth and Enosh what the intruders were saying about their true intentions.

The preachers replied, "We are not taken by surprise by that serpent's schemes, but you can be sure that God will preserve His people and the Seed."

"Oh thank God," the man said.

As expected the older people in the communities often disapproved of the growing trend and they began getting louder in resistance to these ungodly unions. "God is not joining these two as one, this is unnatural and sure to bring about the destruction of our future," was their protest.

A town hall meeting was held later in the week after a breakout of wedding ceremonies were held. These concerns were to be properly addressed at that venue. "What are these so-called ministers doing by officiating these wedding ceremonies? I don't think they give the slightest care about anything that the circuit preachers say. I think the ministers are doing it all just for the money."

The younger generation of kids that attended the meeting

simply disregarded their elder's warnings as, "old fashioned, narrow minded and archaic thinking that is not in keeping with the new and preferred way to move forward." The giants meanwhile did not care one bit now that their dominance was established and they continued to be very productive and fruitful.

"While we debate the morality of all of this, said the town mayor, there are many children of this new breed being born."

One of the new mothers in attendance took offence at the mayor for referring to her son as "this new breed," and publicly dressed him down over his remarks.

Satan was unnoticed as he sat in the back row of the crowded town hall center but he listened intently to every word. A couple hours later he met up with Anak to recount all the meetings events. "Ha, Satan laughed as he saw the growing trend, be fruitful and multiply, sure just not after their own kind."

The thread of this strategy wove its way through each relationship until it became the fabric of society, causing a deluge of demonic genetics flooding into the human bloodline as a result.

What came from these unions was half human and half Rephaim. In future references of them, they were called Nephilim, descendants of Anak.

"Let's see if the Seed can come now since it won't be long until every living being on earth is fathered by demons. Ha, funny, guess whose son he will be. The Seed that is going to be the Savior of the world will be my son," and Satan laughed and laughed as he stood there in his iconic pose.

The offspring with the new strand of DNA were very large as the Nephilim proved to be progenitors of children that were much larger than those that were born fully human. Growing to heights anywhere from 15 to 22 feet tall as adults, they toward over their human counterparts. "Just how many they can produce through their entire lives and what size each of them will be remains to be seen, it appears that someday everyone is going to look like them," said one concerned old man. "It all depends on how many women each one can impregnate each year," said his disheartened friend.

Of course, not every single newborn would grow to huge proportions. Much of the determining factor in their adult size was dependent upon how much DNA was dominant from the mother's traits. Some babies were very large and others were not nearly as big as the largest. "All that matters to me, said Satan, is not the final size of those born but the fact that theirs and the entire human blood line was being filled with demonic DNA. Let the Seed try to come through those genetics." Every time he saw the apparent success of his unfolding plan he laughed hysterically. It seemed to many of his fallen comrades that lord Satan was always laughing these days, "like some kind of joker." This sensation of laughter prompted him to make his presence known more readily and openly in public than he ever thought would be possible. "Now everyone is either glad to see me or has resigned themselves to their fate and accepts my presence as normal. Things are going even better than I ever thought they would," he said to Reph.

The demon giants gradually disregarded all cordiality as their successes mounted. Finally, they were no longer gentle or patient at all in selecting the daughters of Eve that they preferred. Knowing that resistance to their desires was futile, they just began going into houses and taking the women that they wanted to mate with. Anak told his associate Reph, "There has been no one strong enough among the humans that can stop us from doing what we want. Of course, you desire their daughter so why go through the formality and waiting to marry one when all you want to do it spread your seed. Just go into her room and take whichever one you want, it's that simple." Sometimes the startled girl would scream for help. Anyone who would come and try to hinder the giant's progress would always be met with destruction. News circulated about the father and four sons that unsuccessfully fought a giant that was absconding with the daughter. The men were well armed with knives, clubs, swords and a spear, but these did little damage to the Nephilim. During the fight that ensued the intruder took the weapons from them which he then used to kill each one. It was a gruesome scene that the kidnapper left behind, as if he was leaving a message for anyone intent on following him. As this story was circulating through all the communities it didn't take long for it to become common knowledge that there was nothing that could be done about it. In fact, this method produced a surprising result that suited the originator of the plan to his great delight. After it became commonly accepted that resistance was futile, the younger ones became even more accepting of the arrangements. Many were surprised to find that in time the captive women even preferred the thought of betrothing the Nephilim. "That is probably due to the girls knowing that their fate is sealed once they get captured," two grieving fathers lamented together.

"Everything continues to go according to the plan and with great success, Lust commented, a horde of humans have been born with a mixture of Rephaim and Adamic genes." "Oh yes, I can now see sons of ours in every town and everywhere I go," finished Reph.

Satan's secret weapons were drastically changing the worldwide population. The people no longer resisted the Nephilim, the desire to seek and please Yahweh was waning and the human gene pool was past the breaking point of genetic purity.

The world was no longer on fire with the joy of seeking God. The crowds at the revival services were much smaller than they used to ever be. Angus said to his partner Ghengus, "The enemy seems to be running away with His tail between His legs."

"Soon there will be no sign of Him anywhere, we sure stomped the camel and his nose, lord Satan is brilliant. We are winning without a fight" Ghengus replied and they laughed hysterically.

Seth had passed away, his father Adam had also passed away. Both were carried into the presence of their heavenly Father like Abel and Eve before them. Enosh was still running the circuit but he had encountered so many huge obstacles. Local rulers of the towns that he preached in had taken up a strong alliances with the Nephilim against him. All freedom of expression and of religion had been greatly curtailed. He had to watch what he said from the pulpit and also when giving his counsel to any struggling adherent.

On more than one occasion he spent a night or two in the town stocks or even a dungeon for speaking the truth. The magistrates deemed his comments as hate speech for speaking out against the Sons of Anak and their activities. "They have more rights than you do, Mr. Preacher," they would say to him as they slammed his jail cell door shut. "Quit offending everyone with your talk of sin and sinners, God, righteousness, judgment, heaven and hell. How do you know anyway?"

One night after comforting a distraught member of his dwindling crowds, that person went to the local authorities to expose Enosh's comments. "The preacher said the giants are a race of devils and that anyone with their blood in them is infected and beyond hope," she told them. "Is he still making those comments, won't he ever learn?" A judge said to her, "Since Mr. Enosh has not responded accordingly to our way of thinking, we will show him our new method of changing people's minds." For this they lowered him down into a muddy cistern where he stayed three days and three nights. Finally, a servant boy from the magistrate's office lowered a rope made from sheets that were tied together to lift the exhausted preacher out of the mire.

"The tide of evil is building but God did hear the constant cries for justice from those who stayed true to Him. He is going to answer but only in the fullness of time," a confident Enosh assured the magistrate before he shook the dust off of his shoes in front of him and then he left that town.

The passage of years alone on the circuit and the harsh persecutions that he endured rendered Enosh to be old and infirm. He had a son, Kenen, born to him when he was 90 years old. For a time Seth, Enosh and young Kenen had the duo operating as a trio. At the height of their influence, years ago, Kenen was youthful but showed great promise in the ministry. His presence alone brought an even greater excitement in the crowds while he was on the stage. He added so much to the message of his father and grandfather but more than that he brought the youth out to the meetings and oh did those young ones in the crowd get excited. They liked listening to the elder preachers but "we really came out to see and hear the young one," many said. Kenen made sure to never disappoint them.

As the years of work and influence with his father stacked up, unfortunately, so did the legal problems. The authorities felt that the time for them to campaign openly against the preachers had come. "I am sure that we will have enough community support to push for the criminalization of their hate speech. The crowds have greatly diminished and the preacher's power and influence is no longer a concern to me," said the magistrate.

Enosh and his son knew that they had reached their high watermark some time ago. It was apparent that the trio and their influence has been slowly but steadily declining since Seth's passing. Enosh told Kenen that in spite of this he "wanted to finish his life's mission of encouraging the people of God to stay faithful in preaching God's word to a sick and darkened world.

I will continue until the Lord comes to get me no matter what the leaders do to me,"he said. Kenan answered, "I no longer see things this way father, I cannot go with you any longer, I have decided to move on to another vocation while I am still young enough to succeed." With a little bit of history of his own under his belt, and with the passage of time, Kenen said, "I have learned of another undeniable fact of this life: things change. Father I must leave this line of work although I know it is critical to be done, he told him, I have a wife and young ones that depend upon me as I did on you. Times have changed since those days. Back then we didn't get thrown into cisterns for days and have to pay huge fines for what they deem to be incorrect speech. I am returning to full time work as a rancher on our estate. I will continue to support you with funds and donations, but I am needed at home." With that declaration Kenan left his father and the ministry to tend to his own house with family and oxen shortly after this conversation. He concluded, "father, like the ocean tide, good fortune rises up and drops back down. There is a constant ebb and flow between good times and trying times, between prosperity and lack that no man can alter."

"I understand son, said Enosh, but before you leave, I must entrust the archive to you. As you know it has been passed down through our family line beginning with Adam and must continue forever. Be faithful to record what God is doing in the world. He is working to bring the Seed and He will come. The serpents head will be crushed although now it seems hopeless. Be strong Kenen and in time you will pass this history onto your chosen son to be the witness." Along with Kenen's preaching ministry, his father Enosh also died. He was 905 years old at his end and after that there seemed to be no one willing or able to keep the preaching circuit alive, but Kenen kept the book.

CHAPTER FIVE

With the passage of more time the effect of the Nephilim's presence had taken an even more pervasive hold on the entire world. As a result of their full-on assault on the genetic pool of the sons of Adam and daughters of men, fewer and fewer full-blooded sons and daughters of Eve were born. The societal trend was that less and less offspring were born pure blooded, free from the effects and defects of the satanic gene pool. Lust commented to Anak, "as a result of the continued employment of this demonic strategy there are many more sons of Anak on the earth now than there are sons and daughters of Adam." Anak responded, "No one knows for sure what the percentages are of each group in the world, he paused, it just seems to most of us that the Nephilim are everywhere." "Indeed, they are," finished Lust.

Kenen put down the book and noted to his family, "a simple glance at any person can quickly and accurately enable the observer to ascertain anyone's ancestry. Sons of Adam are born only through the union of an Adamite and a daughter of Eve. Sons of Anak are also born through the union with a daughter of Eve but their blood traits always prevail over hers so they produce male offspring only. The woman can and does influence the final size of the giant but only by degrees. Another very distinguishing characteristic of their descendants, beyond impressive size, is a very long neck," he added. His daughter quickly picked up on this truth and commented, "the length of their necks is obviously a specific and dominant trait.

When Kenen was 90 years old he fathered Mahalalel. The son chose to follow his father into the agriculture industry which was booming at the time. "Not only do the sons and daughters of Adam need to eat but the Rephaim also love to gorge themselves during meals and they eat much more than we do," Kenen told him. The amount of food that they can consume became legendary within the communities. Kenen continued, "at one feast they are capable of finishing off a banquet table that was created to be more than enough food for five men, all by themselves." This instruction encouraged Mahalalel, "We will always have a steady supply of customers," he added. As a result, the market for food stuff, meat and produce soared in those days. So although many were suffering and the human race was failing because of the Nephilim seed, Kenen and Mahalalel prospered greatly due to the gluttony of the giants. Kenen told his son "the sons of Anak excel in two things: procreating and indulging their massive appetite. We might as well make the most of this evil situation if the Lord wants to bless us in it." Mahalalel stared at his father being now made aware of that connection and nodded his head, "that's right, we should just keep doing that."

The skills of raising a crop and getting the produce to market became streamlined on Kenen's estate. The customary waste and loss of seed and product that had always been accepted as normal was cut way down. This also redounded to the pleasure of Kenen and his family. Although he at times felt terrible for leaving his father on his own on the circuit during the years before he died, and not continuing as his co-worker, Kenen also was convinced that he "was blessed by God because of the earlier work he did do as a member of the trio." More than that he "was sure that his many blessings were more a result of his father's and grandfather's faithfulness than his own and how he often supported his father's work with bountiful gifts of supplies and money," he often taught Mahalalel. The father also taught his boy many other lessons as well on successful farming. Most importantly, he told him regularly, "to stay pure and have nothing to do with the sons of Anak, other than feeding them."

Through the years Kenen watched Mahalalel grow, prosper and take on the responsibility of tracking the family lineage and purity. He was sure that the book was to go into his hands so at his old age, when he was infirm and not sure how much longer he had, he commissioned his son to keep the book. "My father passed this record on to me just as his passed it on to him. We have all kept the book as we should, now I am passing this all-important task on to you, Mahalalel. Read through it and take good care of it. It is our family testimony to the work of God and it will save mankind. We are living in dire times of ever growing evil. Purity from entanglements with the Nephilim and this book are your two most essential responsibilities. There are many improvements that must be made to the oral and this written tradition that this book contains, be sure that you make them. As you have more children be sure to pass this task on to the chosen son, do you accept this commission?" His son replied, "I am the right man and I will follow your instructions zealously. "Shortly after commissioning Mahalalel Kenen died. He was 910 years old.

When Mahalalel was 65 years old, he fathered Jared. He taught his son all of the essential truths that were passed on to him by his father, Kenen. The most important lessons that Jared learned from his dad was knowing, "that without a close relationship with El Olam, the everlasting God, he wasn't any better than the giants," Mahalalel often repeated this to his own son. Early on in Jared's life Mahalalel knew that his son was the one to keep the book after him. He also observed that "he has a talent for business and agriculture, I will turn the company over to him now and the book to him, as well, afterward."

When control of the sprawling ranch was deeded over to him, Jared managed to add much more land to it and value to the estate. Jared also realized that hiring men, and not just family members, to labor in his business was very cost effective. He could go to bed and have his men continue to cultivate and bring in the crop as he slept. He continued to make money on the sale that was the inevitable result. Because of his ingenuity Jared had much more time to focus on his spiritual life than his father, Mahalalel, ever did. He learned to leverage his time and use new forms of technology in the field and human nature in the marketplace to his family's benefit. He then established a greater connection with the Maker and recorded everything from the beginning to the current day in the book. Up until then his family had much more unrecorded history that was taught, rehearsed and passed down to all and recorded by a chosen son in the family. It still needed to be added to the book which was also in much need of updated organization and reprint as the years have taken their toll on the original version of the archive. The father had long ago become firmly convinced of Jared's ability to fulfill this obligation, as well, having been so faithful with the family business and he was never disappointed by this decision. Jared in turn wrote every necessary event down. He took great pride in the improvements that he made to the registry. He verified all the facts that he recorded so that he could account for them with certitude. What he wrote down and passed on was correct.

"When the time is right, I will pass the keeping of the archive on to my own chosen son," he said to Mahalalel.

When Jared was 162 years old, he fathered Enoch. As Jared

continued to spend more and more of his time seeking to know Adam's Maker, he became more influential to his son Enoch. Of all the activities that Jared was involved in during each day, the most important to him were the hours that he spent with Jehovah. That time was precious to both him and to Enoch who also was drawing closer. Enoch watched his father withdraw each afternoon from the activities of his family business to pray and reflect. Wanting his own fellowship with the Lord he too found his own private place and began to retreat there in order to call on the name of Yahweh. Most youths of his day and age liked to spend their time chasing girls and tormenting the Nephilim, but Enoch was other worldly minded. He seemed to only think of the great city that he said was "somewhere in heaven." In his young adulthood he demonstrated a shrewd propensity toward understanding who God is and that He has a plan for the earth. The things he would talk about would often startle and amaze each family member. His mother often asked him, "how do you know these things, son? and that such wonderful and terrible things will happen?" He explained how, "the Maker of the plan enables me to see into the future through visions which are so clear to me that I can hardly move for quite a while after the viewing." Many, many things were shown to him in this way. His family came to trust him and would ask him for more detail about the Lord's plan. Enoch began to realize that he was becoming an important spiritual leader in his family. *When the time for me to be entrusted with the registry finally arrives, I am going to be very careful to record each vision exactly as I saw them, within that book, he thought.*

More visions came to Enoch as he would sit and stare in stunned silence at the prospect of what he saw coming. "It left me full of awe, it was devastating," he would explain to his family later. He recorded his visions in one book and the record of God's acts in the family registry.

Enoch was fast becoming a changed man because of all these visions. His knowledge was transforming him into a person with a single purpose in his life. Enoch was also becoming very well known as the "one that will restore the old paths."

One day the young man told his father that, "I was called to be a prophet, I have to leave the farm and head back to the old circuit." Jared understood full well, "I have seen the changes taking place in you, son, and I also know the One that is transforming your life," he said. "I guess I should have known this day would come and this news should have come as no surprise to me."

"Be careful, he advised Enoch, there are so many Nephilim out there and the old warn path is overgrown and abandoned. It will require a lot of work to cut it all back and clear it again. They are sure to notice you and what you are doing."

"I am prepared to work, preach, pray and die, he replied to his father. What can they do to me since I do not fear them?"

The following day Jared and Enoch began to prepare for his departure. "Here you go son, Jared said, take these two pack mules, take more if you think that you will need them. We will load both mules up with everything that you will need that we can think of."

It took a few more days to be sure that he had everything that would be necessary to complete his mission. Enoch went over his packing inventory one last time. "Plenty of food, water, clothing, sheltering supplies, tools to dig, cut, and build with, as well as to study, write, and preach with. Provender for the animals, equipment to service their needs. I think it's all in there," he said.

"You know, son, you will never be back to manage the ranch, ever again, I am sure this is a lifelong decision for you with no turning back." Jared said.

With tears in his eyes Enoch and his loving father walked

together to the family feast that was being given in Enoch's honor. His family was letting him know how they loved him so and that they support his new life mission. "He could stay here and have a life so comfortable and nice, his mother said, but he must be about his Lord's business." After a long and bittersweet feast, Enoch gave a hug to each family member at the dinner, then he went out to the mules. He was a young man then but figured all along that this was his calling for the rest of his life. He would be back to raise a family of his own but never as the son that was in line to take over family business operations. Jared was the only one who could bear to watch as Enoch and the animals slowly melted into the horizon. There was only one possession on those heavily laden animals that, father and son agreed, needed to change hands before he left and go with him everywhere: the book. The next leg in the journey of this historical archive belonged solely to Enoch now.

After a couple of days of walking with the mules Enoch and his pack animals arrived at the first town on his destination. He led the animals to an old shed where they could rest a few days before commencing his destiny. He went out to the wilderness to look for the trail head that used to open up the road to the meeting sight. After a long excavation of the foliage Enoch discover the remnants of the old monument that pointed the way to the old camp site. His heart began to race and his hands began to move franticly as he pulled the overgrowth away to form a clearing. Later that evening he could finally step onto the roadway that he was looking for and he knew the real journey was soon to begin.

It didn't take him long to realize that the path to his calling was choked out by years of neglect, overgrowth and vandalism.

Most of the roads and trails that he attempted to go down on the old preaching circuit had been allowed to fall into disrepair from neglect. The authorities purposely abandoned them so that they would never be used again.

"To me, those locations were not historical landmarks to be preserved, but blotches on the shared human and inhuman destiny," said one of the resource managers.

None of the opinions of the government officials mattered to Enoch, however. From the lowest intern all the way to the king in charge, Enoch was not the least bit concerned of their desire to destroy the old paths. He was filled with a holy fervor. An eternal message was oozing from the very pores of his skin. He was certain that *if I do not preach the vision, that it would consume me like a fire.* He was certain that if God didn't strike him down for not following the call, the withholding of the message inside of him would. *I am* determined *that none of that is going to happen to me, he thought.*

As his hard chopping, sawing, raking and clearing and building work continued he saw his chance to proclaim his messages *where the multitudes used to gather by the tens of thousands during the revival services.* The old platform was past repair, so he made a new one. *A couple days of industrious labor and I'll have this place ready to go, he said to his mules.*

Enoch intended to spend the rest of his nights out in the open, on or along the circuit. "We won't be needing any lodging in the towns, we got all that we need in the bags," the mules just stared at him.

"Look, the Lord is coming with 10,000s of His holy ones," his message rang out on the first day. All day and into the night Enoch prophesied. At the beginning there were only small crowds of five or 10 people. In time, however, those numbers doubled and grew even more.

People love to watch a fire burn, he thought. Enoch did not worry about the numbers of his audience. He only cared about his God and doing what he was compelled to do. *I plant the seeds and God has to water them and make them grow,* he reasoned. He was going to fill the airwaves with his voice and, in so doing, give glory to his God. *The people who come to hear it must be drawn here by God,* he concluded.

"They are coming, to execute judgment on all and convict all the ungodly of their deeds of ungodliness committed against Him."

The town mayor heard of the new preacher and determined to go out to see and hear him. The mayor commented shortly after attending one of Enoch's rallies, "once again the preachers are getting themselves into trouble." One of the local authorities concurred. "The giants really will not like hearing this one bit," he said. Of course, their fellow bureaucrats agreed with them. "It has been so long since any of us has had to deal with any of those pesky preachers. I thought they were all dead and gone for good. What does that silly fool hope to gain by stirring up a hornet's nest?" The local's rulers were in a planning meeting on how to stop this firebrand from going any further in polluting the minds of others with this "hate filled rhetoric."

"We only have got to warn him and threaten him to stop, that should end this before it becomes more of an issue to us. Hopefully that is all it is going to take," the sheriff stated. "Go ahead and send the new guy to go threaten him. I anticipate that this rich young preacher is smart enough to listen to reason for his own good."

"We will do that but none of that preacher's forefathers ever stopped when we told them to," replied the deputy.

"Oh geez, that's just great. I didn't know he is from that peculiar family of separatists," cried the sheriff.

A few hours later Enoch graciously listened to the most recently employed constable as he repeated his threat against him, just like he was instructed to do. The preacher politely declined and continued his sermon anyway.

"The mayor said to tell you that your freedom and livelihood are at risk from the giants if you continue this illegal activity," he finished.

While the messenger was still on the platform with him, Enoch returned to his sermon: "He is coming to punish ungodly sinners for the ungodly things they have spoken harshly against Him. They are foul mouthed, grumblers, and seek only to fulfill their sinful desires," his sermon continued. Many of the attendees questioned if the police force was joining the preaching circuit too, having seen that their man was up there on the platform with Enoch.

"Now he is directly referring to us and not just the Anakim," bellowed the sheriff. He did not like being the butt of this wild looking preacher's sermon material, not one bit. Pressure from the authorities was beginning to build on Enoch.

"Cease and desist" came the command as they posted the order right on to his preaching platform. During his next service the crowds were getting even larger. More and more people kept coming to hear this new message and see what the authorities were going to do. In the middle of a sentence Enoch looked down at the crowd and noticed the paper note tacked to his platform. He smiled as he picked up the one-page document that had his picture on it. He thought it was very funny. "Do you think this drawing looks like me?" "They can't possibly be talking about me; I'm way better looking than this fellow." As he turned the page around to show it to the crowd, raucous laughter came back in response from his followers. "The crowds might not be quite as large as they used to get when the trio preached, but Enoch is becoming very famous, said the deputy. Everyone knows of that wild-eyed book thumper that preaches judgment, damnation and turning your heart back to God."

By this time in his ministry he had gone a long time without a haircut or a shave. The clothes that he left the estate with so long ago had worn out and he was now used to wearing outfits he made entirely out of camel hides and raccoon pelts.

Finally, the rulers had enough of him and decided that Enoch had to be done away with for good. They counseled together long and exhaustively over the best way to do it. "Obviously he is not going to stop just because we told him to, a clerk lamented, but I know a man," he continued. Ultimately, they decided to pay that man who was expert in the field of assassination. This man was known for his ability to get in close to his target in order to inflict a mysterious cause of death. He was equally as adept at ending someone's life without anyone ever even knowing he was there. He had his tricks of the trade down to an art form and he possessed every means and the know how to use them. "Does anyone even know where this fellow lives or where he comes from?" the magistrate asked before they wrote the contract for the hit.

The unnamed assailant was careful, patient, and above all cautious. He meticulously plotted out his way in and out of the jobs for which he was hired to perform. The government leaders kicked in a little extra "kitty" for him seeing that Enoch was such a high value target and they wanted the job to be a priority.

The authorities wanted Enoch dead and for it to be done quickly and without any mess. Some, they hoped, might conclude from the look of no foul play that God Himself struck Enoch down. "We are giving you a little extra, to make sure that this delicate matter is handled in a clean, professional and timely manner," said the notary. The assassin just smiled wryly at him.

"Wouldn't that be a funny twist? The preacher that preached damnation to sinners was damned as a sinner that didn't listen to his own preaching." They all laughed together as the assassin left the room. "We'll have to advance that speculation in the aftermath," they all agreed.

In the back of the room was the one who trained and advised the assassin, his forked tongue kept darting in and out of his mouth, he also smiled wryly.

Enoch had been a preacher for hundreds of years. Shortly after his 365th birthday he planned on conducting the largest, most expansive revival service of his career. He said, "That I am going to shake the very gates of death right off of their foundations. I will call the series of lessons, the Gate Shaking Series," and he laughed. His mules just stared at him again. He still did not know that he was a high-priced target. The assassin was just not able to get the angle on Enoch that he was continually trying for. Still, Enoch had no reliable help, but he always told himself that *I do not need help from man. God is my helper.*

Sometimes while he was away from home for extremely long stretches of time Enoch would reflect on his many happy memories of the family. "I am especially grateful for my son that helped me draw even closer to Yahweh through greater devotion. I know that my walk with God is much more personal than ever before since his birth, for that I am exceedingly glad. There is something very special about that baby and it has taken a profound hold on me," he said.

Methuselah was born when Enoch was 65 years old, this little boy really sparked an even greater fervor for the everlasting in the heart and mind of the prophet. Methuselah's father gave him his name in order to signify the worldwide watery catastrophe that will occur shortly after his death. No one knew when Methuselah would eventually pass away, but Enoch knew what will happen after he did. "I have to include this latest revelation in my chronical next time I am on the circuit. The day and the hour of Methuselah's passing can no man know. You can be sure that it is appointed unto all men to die, and after that, to face the judgement of God, he preached. He will die as we all must, but woe to him that does not prepare for that calamitous day." Enoch was now satisfied that he knew how the judgment, of which he warned, would be carried out. When his son dies God will shortly after flood the whole world with water. Exactly how to express the deluge was a little beyond his insight. He was just not going to be able to give all of the full details to the listeners or record them in the book. "Eye has not seen nor any ear heard or mind conceived of the things that God has in store," he proclaimed.

With this added insight inserted into his sermon the authorities became even more uncomfortable. They passed the pressure that they were feeling onto the assassin. "Now he is saying that we are the cause of the judgements that he says are coming, get the job done, they demanded, or you will be taking his place." Little did they know at that time that they would never hear from Enoch again.

Prior to departing, very early in the morning, on what would be his last day of work, Enoch recorded his entire prophecy about his son, his great grandson Noah, and the flood in the archive. Later that afternoon, just before he left the house he handed the book to Methuselah and explained to him what his role will be in its continuation. "In time you also will pass this assignment onto your son, Lamech, who will in time pass it onto to his son. "Methuselah understood completely and accepted the assignment with all gravity but with concern. He had watched his father many times as he sat with the book open in front of him while writing in it. He was worried about the upcoming trip and had to express his fears to his father. "Father there are so many Nephilim out there now, I am worried that one of them might try to get you while you are away, let me come with you. What will we do without you if you don't make it back?"

Enoch answered, "son, you belong here to run the business, besides we serve a mighty God. If He is for us, who can be against us? Our God is able to turn those giants into hamburgers if He wants to and I will eat them." Both father and son broke out into spontaneous laughter and had to hold each other up to keep from falling down in hilarity. "That was a good one dad. You are so funny. I will miss you until you get home." Enoch hugged Methuselah, Lamech, Noah and the rest of his family with a real embrace and then he spoke directly to his great grandson before he left for his trip. "You might be the one to carry the book through the flood into the new world. If Methuselah lives as long as his forefathers did you will be of age to receive the call, prepare yourself. You have great favor with God. "Noah simply replied, "yes grandfather."

Now Enoch was totally confident that everything was going to be just fine. He knew that his family and the archive were in the right hands. Enoch said goodbye and they never saw him again.

Lamech listened to what his grandfather told his son and a spark was lit in his spirit. Beyond running the family business, Lamech suddenly realized that had a new mission in his life. He had to prepare Noah for his own life purpose. Noah also was appointed to be the eventual keeper of the historical archives from a young age but he was going to do much more than that, he was a special boy.

Assassin understood exactly what the authorities meant when they told him to "hurry up and get the job done." As soon as he left their presence, he went to stake out Enoch. "I know his circuit now; I know where he has been on this his latest stop and where he still has to go to complete his mission. I can deduce what his next location will be and I will get there before him to make sure it is his last stop," he told his lord.

Not long after that, Assassin picked the ideal spot from where he would kill Enoch. Eventually his target arrived. *Perfect*, thought the assailant. As he snuck up on him to get within striking distance, a loud roar came crashing down upon them from heaven. Instantly Assassin was thrown into the distance as if flicked away by a powerful finger. He was hurled headlong into the far-off weeds and upon landing he turned toward his target again to consider another attempt.

"You can't take him away from me, I have a job to do and it must be complete," he yelled into the sky as Enoch was picked up by the huge hand and taken into the heavens. Enoch and the hand elevated to greater heights and passed through the opening in the clouds, which then sealed shut as if no disturbance ever occurred.

A bewildered Assassin sat there trying to figure out what he just saw.

"No one would believe this if I tell it to them," he said audibly to himself. "I better not waste any time getting this information to lord Satan, but not before I collect my bounty." *Either way, the preaching comes to an end here today*, he thought,

The crowd had assembled according to schedule, but they were getting restless. "When will he arrive and get this service started?" they all murmured. After waiting for over an hour for Enoch to arrive, they all started leaking away as they realized that he was not going to preach tonight. Finally, the crowd dispersed.

The authorities were satisfied that the job was done as they proclaimed to each other, "we better pay the man," as Assassin held out his hand.

Days turned into weeks and still there was no sign of Enoch. No one, but Assassin knew that he had been translated into heaven. There was no one anywhere near him when God took him. No one else but the officials knew that no one will ever see Enoch again.

CHAPTER SIX

Methuselah had grown worried from waiting for his father to return home from his mission. "Father is long overdue; I fear that something might have gone very wrong for him. He should have been back over a week ago, he told Lamech. I need to know what happened to him. He has never been gone this long past his expected return date."

"We also have been thinking that something must be wrong. We have got to go search for him, he would never go this long past schedule without returning to restock and rebuild his supplies," replied Lamech and Noah.

Every day during Enoch's prolonged absence the three men got up early, asked God for guidance, and went out on the circuit trail to search for him. They frequently had some of their hired ranch hands form a posse to help in the search. "Let's break up into three groups, Methuselah said, and fan out to cover a larger area. Do not be in so much of a hurry that you miss some clues that might tell us where he is, and don't forget to bring some of the hounds."

"We will do exactly as you say, boss," Lamech, Noah and the leaders of each group consented before they all rode away.

Even though all three parties consisted of excellent trackers, not a single group or individual ever found any sign of Enoch's whereabouts. Methuselah was nevertheless convinced of his eventual success. He thought his rounds needed to expand drastically and cover more area. "Methuselah said he was going to his father's circuit and then out to the far country, out further than he has ever been before, he reminded them. I must push the limits of this search to the distant lands. This was my father's grandest plan, to bring the message to the outer limits"

Methuselah decided to ride the fastest steed in the herd. He was going to go out way beyond the extreme lands where tales of very large animals came from. "I'm going way farther than my father's circuit ever took him, that's where he said he was heading."

"Are you sure you want to go out into that territory, boss?" His men said. "Everyone knows the cave people hunt the behemoth out there."

"It is possible that my father pushed the boundaries of his ministry way out into those unknown locations. If I must, I can hire one of those cave dwellers as a guide. Perhaps one or more of them even went to some of his gatherings when he was near their area."

His associate replied, "There are likely to be hostile people in the lands that are outlying areas. I agree that in those locales something unknown could have overtaken him since he was not familiar with the area or the inhabitants, do you want me to go too?"

"God forbid, yet I have to know what happened, just my horse and I will be going to the outer frontier," the boss said as he rode off quickly.

The first two days on his search didn't produce any new clues. The third day of his campaign figured to do the same as it was coming to a close until suddenly Methuselah was struck with a very bright vision as he rested against a large rock.

There he is, Methuselah saw him, *just as plain as day.* Methuselah couldn't tell for certain that it was just a vision, it seemed so real. He witnessed his father's departure from earth as if the event replayed right before his face. Methuselah saw the whole scene unfold before his very "eyes." Did the vision take minutes to view or was it hours? he didn't know. But he was sure that he saw Enoch leave earth clutched in the midst of a giant mighty hand and straight into glory he rose.

The dazed man finally regained his senses as he slowly came back to consciousness and his foremost thought was, *the book.*

The realization of what happened to his father hit him hard before he had an opportunity to record the apparition. "Oh my God, why did this happen? What are we going to do now that father Enoch has been taken from us?" He stuttered to himself. He decided to leave that location and head for the ranch as soon as the sun comes up. At first it seemed to him that it was a terrible thing that was done to such a righteous man. "Why did God do that to him and to us?" the questions continued. As he rode the stallion home, his mind could not get off of the thought: *what am I going to do now? My trusted mentor and best friend is gone.* All at once and without warning or prior notice, his father Enoch was not on earth any longer, Methuselah was very sure of this. *I must be the same for my sons as my father was for me.* There was still a long way to ride to cover the vast distance back to his home. He turned his thinking, momentarily, to his future. He figured "the best thing to do would be to get back into running the estate and help my sons and grandsons get married and raise a family of their own, he said to his horse. The first thing that I have to do is find only pure daughters of Eve for them and then have them get married." *They are all young and good-looking and have lots of money, we all have lots of money.*

There was quite an uproar upon his arrival at the estate and Methuselah told everyone what actually happened to Enoch and what his new family plan will be. All who heard him were in awe and agreed, "we are living in very important times," they said.

Methuselah had no idea that it would be so hard to find some pure women. The giant's agenda was still spreading like

Multiflora Rose bushes. To that point he never really paid much attention to what was happening all around him. *Until now I never gave any thought to how difficult the Nephilim are making it to find a wife and have a family.* Although he knew all along what the Anakim were doing, the extent of their success was never apparent to him before. Nevertheless, he was committed to this principle as keeper of the sacred archive. "I will never settle for a daughter that has been with an Anakim or a mixture of the two species to share in our bloodline, he told his entire family. Now is the time to find a spouse, for soon there might be no one left for us. This search will go on for as long as it is necessary. I just never imagined that it would take so long, he said, but I am certain of eventual success."

"We will all help you brother, each one of our grandsons will have a pure wife," his older sister assured him.

CHAPTER SEVEN

Many of the community businesses at that time were in the practice of employing a number of the sons of Anak in their line of work. For the most part, the giants had a good reputation as hard workers that wanted to keep their jobs. None, however, worked anywhere in the Methuselah Company and this fact did not go unnoticed to the Nephilim. Eventually they became angry about it and began to apply social pressure on the family and their establishment. In spite of this, Methuselah committed himself, all the more, to being faithful to his God. He wanted nothing, for himself and family, to do with mixing with them or their god. "Keep it just business," he told them all.

"That's alright, said Anak to lord Satan, we do not have to attack them in order to destroy them and get control of their company. We can wait them out until they wither away like the produce left on the vine because there is no one to pick it."

Satan really liked the way his protégé thought and planned, "you have learned your craft well," he replied. Anak continued, "we will continue to ramp up the pressure on them with a new tactic that I just devised, wait and see what it is," he said.

Shortly after that conversation the giants organized their efforts and resources and stopped frequenting the Methuselah Company altogether. This effort was subsequently called a boycott and it was "going to continue until Methuselah hired 10% of all his employees in that company from sons of Anak," boasted Anak. Methuselah knew that "this is just a ploy toward ultimately getting control of our brand and then become majority owners. This will never happen, I would rather lose it all before I lost any of my precious ones to the Nephilim," he scornfully promised.

Sales of Methuselah Company goods and services began to decline almost immediately after Anak informed Methuselah and his company that the sons of Anak will no longer be patronizing their establishment.

"Not until you show a willingness to hire Nephilim as employees," he promised.

One year later the giants were still not coming back. Sales were way down, work was very slow. Product was backing up and spoiling in the storehouses and many of his employees were leaving their jobs for more gainful and consistent employment elsewhere. It wasn't long after until there was only a few hired helpers left on their payroll besides the family members. They all worked hard and continued to do so, but now it was primarily just so that they could feed themselves. "Now there are only a few armed and valiant guards to protect their precious little ones, noted lord Satan, the fruit is ready to pluck."

As Methuselah's son, Lamech, rose in corporate responsibility, sales and the family prosperity continued its descent. The stalemate with the giants continued and resulted in the eventual death of the family business.

"The boycott is having excellent results, Satan boasted, we are way ahead of expectations. I have got to promote Anak for the way he is handling this matter," he said.

Besides having food on the table, nothing else was the same for the Methuselah Company as before the boycott. The family had fallen on hard times. There appeared to be no suitable solution and no end to their downward spiral. Occasionally one of his sons would ask him to reconsider. "Father, I remember the old days when we were the wealthiest family around."

"Yes but either way we go, if we give into their demands or stay the course, we lose the business. One path leads to death by theft, the other brings death through attrition. One thing that we must not compromise is this: we must never compromise our bloodline," he answered. The entire family was soon to find out that they still had not yet reached the bottom.

By this time in his life, Methuselah had seen it all. There was nothing that was going to take him by surprise and nothing was going to get him to lose his focus on what was truly important. He was raised by a truly great and godly father. A man that was so good that God didn't even let him die. "He just took him, I guess so that they could be together in heaven. Maybe God had some other purpose for him too," he said.

Methuselah had, at one time, the most prosperous business that for years grew and expanded. They were able to afford and enjoy the best that the world had to offer but this did not cause him to re-focus on to lesser things. Now, however, his financial condition was much less enviable to his competitors and there were things that he could no longer fit into their budget. In spite of this reality Methuselah remained the same rock solid man with his eyes set on his one true purpose. He sure hoped *his children would continue to walk the narrow road that leads to true riches. Where moth cannot destroy, thief cannot break in and steal or rust cannot corrode. He surely hoped that Lamech would be faithful and take good care of his holy obligation.*

It finally fell to Lamech to keep the ranch as productive as possible. "I am passing it onto you," his father told him. Lamech was the one who rose up early, never took time off and went to bed late to see to it that failure was not an option. His personality was the driving type. He had to keep the plow blade in the ground and churning up the soil. Whenever he hit a rocky patch or a large boulder in the furrow or in the pathway of his life, he felt it personally. The delays, setbacks, and annoyances that are sure to follow anyone that is trying to go against the trend really bothered him. He was determined to reverse his family's long-standing downward plunge. "In vain I stay up late and toil, it's all for nothing that I wake up early to begin building each day. God has got to help me," Lamech prayed. He took each and every hardship to heart as if the occurrence was an offense sent from the Almighty. "Nothing, he said in disgust, happens by chance so if it happens at all that could only mean that God designed it." His angered seethed and festered as he constantly linked his current difficulties with all of his past disappointments. He blamed God. "I must be destined to failure, marked by God, like Cain, to never be allowed to enjoy the fruit of my labor," he fumed. Things had really gotten to where they were going very badly, but it was all for no fault of his own. "No matter what I do, though, this business trend continues."

Lamech was a smoldering coal ready to inflame into anger at the very perception of any slight or unpleasant event. "It just seems that there is nothing I can do to reverse this trend of misfortune, and whatever I try to do just ends in failure, he said. God, You have got to help me here, or else I will end in destruction," he would shout as he faced the heavens.

"He is ready now, it is time," the Lord decreed in response to Lamech's pain.

One morning before he went back out into the field, Lamech picked up the book and began reading it from the beginning.

He turned all the pages from front to back and read them all. By doing so he grew in perspective. His view of the world and his life's circumstances changed as well. His heart began to soften, "What should God have done, what could He have done? Judgment was warranted, He is not to blame," Lamech said. He read the account of where God cursed the ground in response to the disobedience in the garden. Lamech knew that it was not any different for him, he too is guilty of sin. He slowly began to understand that he is as much to blame as Adam and Eve are, "for we are all sinners, he said. If ever there is a reprieve from the hard sting of the curse- then rejoice in His goodness. If the bite is painful then I must just endure it joyfully." That was his newfound conclusion and the way he was going to live his life hence forth.

He repented, and although he fully expected the same turmoil in bringing the crop to the table, "I am going to be thankful anyway, and start looking at all the blessings in my life that I've overlooked and taken for granted until now," he admitted. He was abandoning bitterness and his self-pity and putting on gladness. "I have a lot to live for and anticipate that my loving heavenly Father will send relief soon just to help take the pressure off of me," he declared.

Just having made this change of heart within himself produced a big difference in his day to day functions and in his emotional stability. He wasn't so quick to fly off the handle anymore as he used to be at the slightest annoyance. Working the ground was still hard labor and required sweat and physical exertion all day long, but now he was at peace. His newfound balance resulted in a happy, more relaxed family setting as well. His wife and kids were now so happy to see him come through the door at the end of a long day. He always tried to have a joke or an amusing story or an interesting lesson for them at his greeting.

His marriage also improved, and he benefited by the change by fathering another son, Noah.

With the restoration of Lamech, the plan for the coming Seed was right on track. None of the demons nor Satan himself understood the impact that the repentance of that one man would have on the future. That joyful servant of God was going to train and promote greater things in his son Noah than what could ever have been done before.

At that time it was also decreed on high that Methuselah was going to learn of a young woman, who would become Noah's wife, who has never been with a man or a giant.

Methuselah finally did hear of a woman that his grandson, Noah, could marry. She also refused all union with the sons of the giants.

"Methuselah thinks that he was looking for her for a long time, God said, some day he will learn that I appointed this meeting long, long ago."

Naamah had decided as a child, at a very young age, that she "would rather die or be celibate than to subject herself and her future family to the ravages of the sons of Anak," she proclaimed to her family. The men in her family: her father, brothers, and the family servants were in total agreement with her. They were all well known for their combat skills and for the success they've had fighting off the giants on many occasions. It was apparent that the Nephilim planned and lost badly during their many campaigns of attacks against her family. These men successfully kept the giants from taking Naamah and tallied up a sizable number of decapitated giant skulls as trophies for their long running prowess. There were so many Nephilim heads on their property that they just piled them up away from the house so they wouldn't attract varmints. Not many men had the ability to do what they kept doing but these sons of Adam were gifted, well trained in the art of fighting and they were always prepared. "Never pee or sleep without your weapons, always stand together," was there motto. The Nephilim, in response, eventually stopped trying to steal Naamah from them after the number of losses became insurmountable. Their defeats were becoming well publicized in many communities. "What is that one and only daughter of Eve going to be able to do anyway? She is not worth the hit to our reputation and the loss of assets that we are now suffering with all these defeats," Anak confessed. "Yeah, just one daughter of Eve that we couldn't get to. What difference will she be able to make?" Reph answered jokingly.

As the news of Methuselah's search for a pure wife for his grandson spread, the prospective bride's brothers heard of it and made it a priority to introduce their sister to Noah. Finally, the two eligible suitors did meet and they were both smitten with each other at first sight. She wondered, "just how is it that he is still so available. He is handsome, very muscular, a gentleman, and still considered to be very land rich. He is also a devotee of Yahweh who created everything," she said to her father. Methuselah and Lamech also could not have been more pleased.

Noah and Naamah enjoyed a whirlwind courting period that culminated in their wedding and marriage. It was a small ceremony with only family and trusted associates in attendance, but everyone was so happy for the two love birds. There was such a glorious feeling during the entire celebration. Many of the guests said, "the joy of the Lord permeates this blessed union."

Afterward, the newlyweds set up housekeeping on Lamech's estate and started working on their future plans. They were both so eager to begin raising their family. Before their first anniversary Naamah gave birth to a daughter. As the years went by, they made great progress toward meeting all the goals in their family plan by having many good looking and wise children. "We can raise up our own community of worshippers," Noah said to Naamah. She laughed in delight. Noah and his wife were always very happy together. Their large family was no longer prosperous, and they no longer had many servants or a thriving business. They knew they didn't need these things for a good life.

The giants' descendants were no longer frequenting and patronizing the outlets where the family's products were sold. Their neighbors who were still alive and remained thought it would be in their own best interest to go along with the boycott. As a result, everybody went to the competition for their needs of produce and large quantities of food. The Nephilim were still looking for revenge, so the boycott and their other tactics were not going to stop until they were fully satisfied. "We have much less contact with the forbidden race as a result of this boycott, said Noah, but we must remain watchful and in full protection mode of the children. The sons of Anak will never stop until they believe they have won this war." The husband and wife were always very vigilant about assuring that they maintained minimal incidental contact with the giants as well. They really did not want any of their children to associate with them at all but realized that they could not prevent it completely. The population of the giants was proliferating and so now they were everywhere.

The Methuselah Company no longer had enough servants to ward off every aggressive advance from the giants. Noah and his wife knew that the Anakim still harbored resentment about losing out on Naamah. There were no more hired men stationed in every strategic place where a watchful eye was needed to protect. On more than a few occasions a group of the men in the family had to rush in to prevent a giant from accosting one of family's daughters. *Strange*, thought Naamah, *how these issues and monsters never go away.*

"I don't know how much longer we can be successful in our battles to protect the girls," Noah said.

He just didn't know that his prayers were always before the Lord and that God was always on time in His plans and answers for His servants.

When Methuselah was 849 years old the Lord counseled with Himself to prioritize the plan for the necessity of preserving the bloodline and sending the Seed.

The Lord then proclaimed to His servants and to Lamech, "My spirit shall not abide in man forever, for he is flesh: his days shall be 120 years. I am sorry that I made man, for every intention of the thoughts of his heart is only evil continually. I will blot out man whom I have created from the face of the earth."

But Noah, when he was 500 years old, found favor in the eyes of the Lord. The Lord said, "man has filled the earth with violence and all flesh everywhere has corrupted their way. But not Noah, for he walks with Me. He remained true to Me along with his wife and three of his sons and their wives. He and his family continued on the straight road of righteousness. They remain pure but do not put their faith in their own righteousness. Each one recognizes their need of a savior from heaven, the Seed."

Noah and his family maintained regular religious observances each week. The ceremony of the sacrifice was paramount to them in the perilous days in which they lived. Each day Noah's soul was tormented by the evil that was all around him. He cried out to his God continuously in his prayer life and waited expectantly for His answer. "How long, oh Lord, until You bring the division between the vile and the good? How much longer must we endure the schemes, wiles, and attacks of the wicked ones? Come down and deliver us, I pray."

One evening, as Noah held the testimony in his hands and was sifting through its pages, God did finally speak to him as he was resting from the hard day of work.

"The end of all flesh is come before Me; for the earth is filled with violence through them; and behold, I will destroy them all with the earth."

Noah took a moment to be sure he was not in a dream or having a vision as his grandfather had in days gone by. He looked around but saw nobody.

God continued to speak: "make an ark out of Gopher wood. Build rooms for you and your sons and your wives. Cover the entire ark, inside and outside, with pitch."

Noah thought to himself, "pitch?' You want me to build an ark and cover it completely in pitch?"

God continued, "these are the dimensions of the size you are to build it: the length of the vessel must be 510 feet, the width shall be 85 feet, and its height must be 51 feet. Put a window up at the top for ventilation, and a large door on the side. Divide the vessel into three floors. It is essential that you follow these details explicitly, failure to do so will result in total destruction."

Noah was having difficulty comprehending what was happening and the job he was being given. *Of course I always felt like I commune with God during worship but that was nothing like this,* he thought.

God heard Noah's thoughts and knew that He had his full attention. He went on with further instructions: "gather food in the ark, enough for you and your family. Behold, I will send flood waters upon the earth to destroy every living thing that has the breath of life. But I will establish My covenant with you. You and your sons and your wife and your son's wives must go into the ark. Bring two of every living creature after its kind into the ark, they shall be male and female. Birds, cattle, every creeping thing, and every other kind of animal. Two of every sort and seven pairs of clean animals will come up to you to keep them alive in the ark. Gather food for them as well, for you will be in the ark for a long time."

Noah was sure now that God was actually talking to him and giving him these directions. He then spoke and confirmed with the Lord all the things he was told and Noah then began formulating ideas as to just how he could possible do everything the Lord commanded him. *After all these years of listening to grandfather talk about this, it's finally going to happen,* thought Noah.

Following the dialogue Noah hurried home but he couldn't get there to his family fast enough. The direct route was the fastest way but at that time of the night it was also the most dangerous. "I assume that God wouldn't let me fall into the hands of thieves, bandits, giants or ravenous beasts." He was God's man that will be used by Him to rebuild after the total annihilation. He again thought of Grandfather Methuselah. With that realization in mind he took the fastest way home without another thought.

"Gather around my sons and our wives for we must have a family meeting. There are hard times coming and we have to make big changes and begin now. We do not know how much time we have before it will be too late for us too." With that announcement everybody began to look alarmed. They all knew that Noah was not one to jest foolishly. "What do you mean by: too late for us too?" His wife asked.

At the family meeting Noah was very provoked but composed in rendering unto them the best account of his dialogue with the Lord and what God said to him.

"Ok honey, you had a conversation with God?" His wife asked.

"Yes, He spoke to me and I heard His voice just like I hear yours right now."

He explained to them "I had taken and made notes in the archive during our interaction, I was very careful to be accurate."

God was very pleased that Noah was careful to do that. Neither He nor Noah was in a hurry to rush through the instructions as understanding them was critical for success. God gave His instructions and patiently waited as Noah wrote them down in the book that was recently passed down to him by his father. As he wrote he repeated the instructions back to God for accuracy. God made sure that he was correct. "This is going to be a very large and long-term venture comprised of many equally important smaller sub projects," the Lord said.

After both partners were satisfied that Noah had full cognition and an accurate recording of all the details in his assignment, God then departed.

Noah emphasized to his family that there was coming a worldwide cataclysm. "This disaster is going to annihilate everything that breathes on the face of the earth. Only those who make it safely into the ark will be spared the disaster," he reiterated. Once his family understood that he was talking about the same things that Methuselah frequently warned of, they put it all together in their own understanding. The whole group discussed the fact that evil rules the day and that judgment is needed. Shem, the oldest son, said "now I understand what grandpa's name signifies. I always thought that was some sort of metaphor." "Ok, we got that down, Ham said, what is this about an ark?"

Noah took out his notes regarding the construction of the ark and its purpose. He detailed the length, width, and height that it had to be. He explained how God gave him those dimensions and He told them what materials they had to build with. "He convinced me that under those conditions the ark would be stable, safe and strong" Noah assured them. He broke down for them the detailed plans of building the ark into three separate levels. He explained about the rooms, their living quarters, the plumbing, ventilation, and the sewage system that would have to be functional. Then he discussed the passengers. They would be the animals. They had to be male and female of every type of animal from birds to bears, snakes to snails, lizards to lions. Every type of animal with the breath of life had to have a male and female on the ark. "All of the animals and us will be on the ark together so there needs to be a system of cages for the assured safety of each species and us," he said.

Next came the subject of food. "There must be a sufficient amount and type for all to eat during their long stay on the ark. Life will never be the same and I guess that is the whole point, he said. God will no longer tolerate the utter sinfulness, the corruption and the Nephilim. He is going to start over and begin with us," he continued.

His wife spoke up: "how long will we be on the ark with all those animals?" Noah had previously calculated that it could possibly be as long as one year from entry into the vessel until everyone disembarks, so they must plan accordingly. Every member in the family continued the conversation by discussing, openly, as many ramifications as they could consider. After quite a long meeting they could no longer think of any other scenarios to consider. The meeting ended and everybody at the family meeting retired to their sleeping quarters for a good night sleep before morning arrived. It was going to be the start of a new life for all of them.

Noah knew that God was going to bless this undertaking with success so he was eager to begin. Upon the rooster's wakeup call on the following morning the first thing that he and his sons did that morning was locate a piece of ground on their property to map out the large project. The men calculated that the dimensions of the flat building space must be 600 x 150 feet. That will provide ample room to construct the vessel along with plenty of space to cut, saw, measure, move, stack, and study, they agreed. They decided to locate a suitable space that was close to their houses so no one would have to waste time in a daily commute. They finally got busy after all the planning. The men then cleared the plot of land of all foliage, trees and rocks and then began to gather their tools. This location was also where the large table with the various sets of blueprints would be located. The table was going to be the intelligence center of the entire operation.

"We will need saws, lots of saws of every imaginable type. We also must to have plenty of hammers, chisels, ax heads, handles, tree nails, boring bits, and measuring instruments from feet to micro inches. Of course we will need lumber, lots of lumber and it has to be a particular kind," said Noah.

Without being sure exactly how or where to start, Shem suggested that they just get started. They decided to cut down a cedar tree and cut it into the pieces that they will need. After the tree was felled Noah went back to the blueprints to plan a course of action. He stated that he knew where to begin so they began cutting and constructing the Keel of the ship from the fallen cedar. The keel was the longest structure on the entire vessel and its most important component. "The keel is essential for the integrity and stability of the ark. It is going to run lengthwise from the back of the ship all the way to the front and up to the top deck. The keel is going to be longer than the ark itself. It will be the foundation upon which every part of the ark gets its strength," Noah explained.

Cedar trees were plentiful in that area of the region and also prized for their beauty and durability. They could grow up to 200 feet tall, but Noah and his sons were looking to use trees that were not so old. The trees that were near 100 feet tall were what they wanted. A tree of that height still had many years of life and growth left and would generally be free of decay, excessive infestation, and defects. "Just look at those beauties, said Ham, I never appreciated cedar trees like I do now. They are incredible. They grow long and straight, perfect to suit the need for the keel." The men would cut down many more trees for the strategically placed stanchions as well. Stanchions would brace up each side of the ark and all three floor levels as well and keep them from sagging. "The stanchions must be placed securely on each floor and be tall enough to reach upward to hold the ceilings above securely in place, explained Japheth. By placing them on the first floor and the second floor they would keep the ship from collapsing onto the deck below it." The men estimated that each stanchion pillar had to be 12"x 12"and 51 feet tall. Shem continued, "strength and stability are the most important elements of each beam for the success of this project. We will also need to cut numerous long studs that will be used for the ribs of the ark. Each rib has to be fastened to the keel and run along the bottom of the hull and then up the side of the vessel all the way to the top of it. Each rib must be perfectly placed and with standard spacing from stern to bow."

"The beams, we will need many beams, and each one must run across the ship from side to side and be supported by the stanchions, said Noah. Their cut length has to be 85 feet. They should be 8"x 8"and placed in such a way as to keep each floor from sagging. We will then nail each floorboard to the beams in order to make the floors," he said.

No one yet knew how many animals there would be or what the combined weight of them on each level would be. "The beams under the floorboards have to be strong enough to hold anything. We have calculated that the ark will need 255 of these specially hewn beams with the specified dimensions placed two feet apart from each other for each floor. The network of the beams will form the trusses. The trusses will run crossways from Port to Starboard and placed from bow to stern and be securely fastened to the framework system and the hull. Each beam truss will weigh approximately 5000 pounds and require a crane boom to lift and lower each one into place. Each crossbeam will then need to be securely fastened to the stanchions system as well and in such a way as to prevent any movement of them." For this purpose, the craftsmen utilized a system of dado joints and large peg and hole finishing system.

After each tree was felled it required a team of 12 oxen and three men to move it from the forest to the processing area. It generally required three days to safely cut each tree and move it to the work site. Twelve more days where needed to process each tree into the required board feet needed to fill each order. Two handled rip saws were the tool of choice for most of the initial cutting on any standing tree. Back and forth the blade would go with a man at each end of the saw. As their arms chugged back and forth in perfect timing each tree eventually fell and would then be processed into logs cut to the necessary specifications.

CHAPTER EIGHT

Once constructing the ark began, it was the only thing that the men and women focused on. Until the day of its final completion they would each work on nothing that was not directly involved with that project's success. "We simply cannot leave anything to chance when it comes to preparing for a successful journey," Noah and his wife reminded them all. The women all agreed to take charge of running the family farm while the men handled the lumber jobs. For the wives waking up each day meant spending hours in the fields. From plowing the furrows to putting the vegetables on the table and everything in between, they did it all. They managed, planned and executed all necessary duties to keep all of them fed and working hard. If the wives ever failed in their objective the entire family could starve. Everyone in the family also knew that if the men failed to complete their objectives that they would all perish in the flood. These ever-mindful facts gave each person all the motivation they needed to be industriously employed each day on their tasks.

The team of men considered specializing in various given jobs, and for some of them, that plan worked wonderfully. When it came to sawing the wood, however, each brother and Noah himself had to produce. At the onset of the project Methuselah and Lamech assisted with the labor. The sound of a saw cutting through timber could be heard all during the business hours for six days a week. No one was able to sustain such a grueling exertion of energy for that long without a break. Lamech was the first one to weaken but he devised a plan to sustain each man's strength. A sawing schedule was implemented in order to save each man's arms and productivity. By it each man knew what days they would be doing the heavy sawing and for the number of hours on those days.

The schedule limited the job to one of the two eight hour shifts per day. That enabled each man one day off from the rigorous activity every other day. No body worked on the seventh day. After a few weeks of working that schedule none of them were lacking in an impressive upper body physique in the neck, back, shoulders, arms and abdominal muscles. Even Methuselah, the eldest, enjoyed taking off his shirt again when it was his shift to make the blade sing. His younger family members loved to raz him about his improved appearance. "Do you see all those women and girls staring at you every time you bare your brawn?" and his son and grandsons would all laugh at the banter. Methuselah would routinely adopt the flexing pose position humorously and kiss both of his biceps in response to the good-natured ribbing. Secretly, he knew that he would not be making the voyage with his family.

Some of the cutting jobs required two men to do. On those projects, where the crosscut saw was used, the team members had to complement each other through the entire cut. Occasionally the kerf in the tree began pinching down on the blade of the "misery whip" as they called it. In those instances, a third man was called on to insert wedges into the cut behind the blade to alleviate the continued pinch. More times than not, however, the whip sang beautifully as it chewed its way through the standing timber. Certain days each week were designated as days for the sawyers to attend to nothing but felling trees and relocating the stripped trunk

The family members were unsure of how long the construction

project would take from start to boarding. The Lord graciously gave them plenty of time to finish the task and they felt on certain days that they were falling behind schedule.

When the trunks of the trees were placed into the processing area the ripsaw was the tool of choice for cutting them into boards. Each cut board had to be twelve feet long and would span six rib trusses when it was put into place on the ark. The same thing was true of the floorboard's going from beam to beam. Each and every finished board had to be smoothed, straight and coated completely with pitch. These requirements were in accordance with the Lord's commands to Noah.

Accessing the pitch and bringing it to the worksite was another project that required careful planning. Japheth stated that he knew of a place that sells it. "We all need to travel together to the Vale of Siddim to collect such a large amount of the sticky black goo and to secure our purchase along the return trip until we arrive back home. Even grandpa Methuselah should come with us since he knows the fastest and safest route that we should take, he said."

His brother Shem questioned whether so many men should leave the estate at the same time to help with this long trip. "The Nephilim are always causing problems for the project. Just because they only vandalize our property doesn't mean they won't attack or do something far worse if they see that we are all gone," he said.

"That is very perceptive, son, but if we don't get the pitch and safely return it back here, we cannot continue the work. We will leave everyone here on full alert while we bring Grandpa with us to speed our journey," said Noah.

"A show of strength by numbers will help us reach a better trade agreement and ward off any would-be thieves and attackers along the way," replied Lamech.

"We are going to have to buy it from the sons of the Zuzims,

THE BATTLE FOR THE SEED

said Japheth, and so we will need to bring horses." "Yes, bring many horses to trade with because the Zuzims never trade fairly," replied Ham. Noah reminded them that "we no longer need so many horses anyway since we have much less need to travel for work purposes."

With the use of ox drawn carts the men brought large vats which to fill up with the trade item and return home with. Each vat was placed in the center of the single axle cart and pulled slowly by an ox. The men paired many vats to occupy the many carts that they brought on the journey. Since the vale was a two-day travel to reach, they wanted to make as few of these trips as possible. Each and every cart and ox that they owned was used on their first trip for hauling. The men decided that they would store the entire inventory in their largest barn after they returned. "We can keep it safely in there until we need it," said Lamech.

The transaction with the sons of Zuzim went well until their leader, Scroozim Zuzim demanded to know why the family needed so much tar. Upon hearing of the construction of the ark every guard and sentry assigned to protect the Zuzim's wealth laughed Noah and his family to scorn. Scroozim Zuzim spoke up after the laughter died down. "For making my day and telling such tales, I will donate one free barrel of tar that you can pour into one of those vats beyond what we trade for. Tell God that it's a donation from me for your voyage." All of his guards and sons broke into laughter again.

Happily, Noah and his sons gladly accepted Mr. Zuzim's generous offer and then departed quickly for the trip home to their family and project.

As the caravan reached the end of their journey the men noticed dark smoke rising in the distance. All at once they stopped to consider what was before them. "That is coming from our land, Methuselah growled. The Nephilim have attacked while we were away. We better double time our speed to stop them from totally destroying everything."

As they drew closer, they saw a raging inferno blazing in the trees of the eastern section of their forest. "If that gets out of control it could ruin the lumber we need to continue building the ark", yelled Shem.

"Easy there son, Noah counseled. If we go barging into that heated mess now, we could all end up as smoking ruins. Only the patch of forest that is on fire will be lost, the rest will be saved because of the fire line that's placed between each section," he said.

Methuselah overheard Noah's reassurances and clarified the situation for his grandson. "Years and years ago I cut swaths of open space between sections of forest to prevent wholescale disaster as in cases like this. At the time it made perfect sense to me although many people thought I was crazy to leave so much land without profitable timber on it. Today that decision is paying off, he yelled. You stay here, I am going to assess the situation," he said.

Methuselah jumped down from his mount and walked quickly toward the smoke. *I might be able to catch the perpetrators that are lingering to watch the blaze if I come up from the southern entrance,* he thought. He instructed everyone to watch for any person that might try to escape being detected upon Methuselah' presence. As they watched from the distance, the men heard Methuselah yelling at someone. "I see you; I knew it was you that did this. You will pay for this treachery and your plan is doomed to fail." Instantly Methuselah jumped backward and then lunged forward in attack on what startled him. There was a large venomous snake that attempted to sink its teeth into his leg. Upon his retaliatory attempt Methuselah barely missed stomping on the serpent's head. In time the snake reared back and returned with a second attempted strike of its own, this time landing upon Methuselah's heel. The men watched helplessly as their patriarch struggled to get away but not without a potentially mortal wound. As the team of family members sped toward their injured member the snake slithered quickly away into the tall grass and beyond.

The brothers stared at each other in fear as their father dismounted to help his grandfather get to his ride. "He got me good this time," said Methuselah.

"We have got to take care of this now or it will be too late, Noah barked. Get me the blade and a leather strap," he commanded. Instantly the eldest son pulled both tools from his own supply bag and jumped down from his horse covering the distance between them by the force of his dismount. Methuselah was already turning pale, but was able to speak. "I tried to stomp the serpent's head but was not powerful enough to finish him off. You can be sure it was him that did this in an attempt to destroy God's plan," his voice trailed off.

"Brace yourself, Noah said as he cut through his grandfather's flesh in an effort to draw the poison out with the flow of blood. Now tie the strap around his leg just below the calf and help me get him on his horse."

"We better get moving, said Japheth. The wives can make a poultice to help draw out any infection."

"Yah," Noah spurred his horse and trod skillfully to the house. The brothers brought up the rear bringing the hard-earned gooey substance the rest of the way.

"Do you think he is going to make it?" asked Japheth.

"He has got to, our project, our very lives depend on it," said Shem.

"You're right, Japheth said, God will not doom us without hope."

"The women will have him resting as comfortably as he can very soon and will have their cures working on him in no time," said Ham.

Once the men realized that their wives knew how to nurse Methuselah back to health they all got back to the work site. They devised a strategy for cooking the goo and coating everything with it. The whole process took much longer than any of them expected but each worker understood how important it was to use the pitch.

With the hot sticky tar they took turns and covered each board completely in pitch, as the Lord said to Noah. Finally, there were many large symmetrical stacks of wood that were prepared and ready for use.

After a beam, board or tree nail was coated it would be relocated back into a stack of material of its kind that was also coated.

This method of cooking, coating and stacking was very effective. When the boards were placed onto their new stack, one inch pegs were then inserted between each row in order to enable the air to circulate throughout the boards and dry all the materials in the pile. Each stack required one full year for seasoning. Once a stack of boards was completely dry the material could then be used in building the project.

Finally, all of the boards and nails were processed, coated and stacked, so the men returned to the sawing schedule in earnest again. The crew was getting in a groove of productivity and systematic progress. As a result of their efficiency, the construction site gradually looked more like an outdoor warehouse. In one area were the many neatly stacked piles of boards and the number of piles was growing by the month. Each stack was twelve feet long, twelve feet wide and twelve feet high resembling a perfect cube. Through the years the number of them became more than an uninvolved on looker could count. Noah and his team always knew how many stacks there was because of their record keeping skills. They always knew the difference between how many they had and how many they still needed. Needless to say, to the local community, this family was obviously more peculiar than the town consensus previously estimated them to be.

Many years of backbreaking work produced everything they needed, much more than they ever thought possible. The cutting, the sawing, more sawing and transporting, the painting, the stacking and restacking, measuring, pounding, holding and so many other jobs were nearing completion. They were getting close to the building phase. Realizing this led to a very sobering for them because they knew that as they began building they also got closer to their destiny. With every thought of their future came another thought of their past. Both subjects often directed the conversations of their daily dialogues. The men loved to reminisce each day of the many times when their wives brought their meals out to them for a momentary break. They could re-taste each memory which, this many years later, seemed to taste even better in their mind. Each member of the crew would eat and fellowship together, being content that this was their whole world, each other. They all relished in it. Not a single one of them longed or wished for anything different. *The job might never get done but we are enjoying each other during this entire process of preparation, thought Noah's wife.* Since each family member joined in this effort they have been totally consumed by its purpose and humanity saving objective. They all agreed that they have already said goodbye to the world and its people; they were not looking back.

"I think that what we are doing is having some impact on those people, Ham said. The other day I heard some of them talking about how happy they were because our project is so good for their economy. They said that tourism has quickly become one of the top three producers of wealth in the area. Of course, they have no idea that their prosperity is only temporary. They all together mock the idea of a worldwide flood."

His brother said, "can anyone tell me what I should expect with this upcoming flood? I see where some of the townsfolk are building houses on hilltops now. Is that all they need to do in order to avoid destruction?"

Noah answered, "The Lord has said that the flood will destroy all flesh. There will not be another living soul or animal on earth that does not first get on the ark with us. Moving to higher ground will accomplish nothing for them."

"OK, but how will it happen, where will all the water come from? There is not enough water on earth to cause the kind of flood that we are preparing for," said his wife.

"The floodgates of heaven will be given expression and all of heaven will voice its approval of this judgement as the flood waters pour out as rain. For 40 days and 40 nights torrents of water will fall from the sky until they cover the earth. All the fountains and springs of the deep, far beneath earth's surface will also be ripped open and thrown aside as the water inside the earth gushes up in mighty torrents. There will be so much water that the tallest giant and animal standing on top of the highest mountain will also be destroyed by the water. They will have no chance of survival, he said. There will be no place for them to go, everything will be wiped out."

"All of those people who keep coming to our gates to heckle and distract us just make it so much easier to cut all ties with this current worldly system," said Ham.

"Don't worry about it, son, that situation is bringing us to the place in our hearts that we should have been all along, separated

90

from the world," Noah replied.

There was so much progress made on the ark that the "people" of the world, as the family called them, frequently came by to watch what the builders were doing. They were always curious to see how many more stacks of painted boards and long beams were added to the already insane numbers of them. Some of the onlookers would occasionally yell out, being unable to help themselves, from making some ridiculous remark.

"Row, row, row your boat
Gently up the stream
merrily, merrily, merrily, merrily
Your life is just a dream."

Everyone who came to watch each day learned the chorus and joined in and then they all would break out into laughter. "They are building a boat to take them away from destruction," the leader yelled. Noah, growing annoyed by the foolishness, looked over at the hecklers and saw a giant elaborately colored man with a forked tongue and very long fingers standing in the front. *I have seen that stranger in the town before.*

Finally, Noah and his sons decided to build a high fence to keep those "people" and the growing crowds at bay. "I think that we should use half of a stack of boards to build a fence so those people can't see what we are doing," said Shem. "I agree, Japheth answered, they are so distracting." Yet as the project continued to progress, so did the numbers in the crowd. The fence ended up being nowhere big enough to secure their total privacy. Noah thought back to the days that he read about in the book, back when his forefathers attracted large numbers like this during their days of running the preaching circuit. "What should we say to them?" asked his oldest son. "Just let your hammer and your tools do the preaching," Noah replied.

With the necessary lumber having been cut and prepared, the next project that was in the blueprint but had yet to be started was the plumbing system. Noah and his sons understood very well that a three-story structure containing people and many more animals had to have a water and sewage arrangement. Water was essential for cleanliness and sanitation as well as dietary needs. With that many thirsty mouths to keep moist and satisfied a simple bucket method would never do. The builders had to utilize technology like what they had in their own homes. This was the only way to be able to keep themselves and their passengers alive through their perilous adventure.

With proper planning and preparation this vital component could be installed. They possessed the technology to make a functional water system that would require only minimal maintenance. "We have never plumbed a system on the scale that this one will need," said Shem at the planning meeting. "That is true, but if we just enlarge our thinking regarding the required solutions we will be very able to produce the size that we need for the job," Lamech answered. With that comment, every member in the group felt confident that this obstacle will also be overcome just like every other one that they have encountered thus far. "Like every other vital system on the ark, the plans for the water system had to be carefully prepared and implemented. In order for the water needs of every living thing that would enter the ark to be supplied, a piping network had to be installed," Lamech continued. Noah said, "my sons and I know how to bore holes through the length of logs and connect them together and make a watertight pipe of any length. We can use pitch to seal the connection points that will not leak. We will hollow out big logs and small ones using different size boring bits and thus be able to make the pipes that can withstand sufficient water pressure. In time we can construct a very sophisticated network of pipes," he said.

It didn't take long before a new stack was added to the lumberyard. Piles and piles of hollowed out long logs began to form in an area of the grounds that previously had been empty. Of course, the sawing schedule did not change but now log boring was added to the list of specialized activities. The men devised and ingenious contraption to get this project completed with the use of minimal manpower. The plan called for using donkeys that were harnessed to a long pole that could turn a hardened drill bit through a system of gears. With proper pressure, the bit will then churn its way straight through the center length of each log attached to it. As they examined the plan, Noah and his sons were very congratulatory to each other over how brilliantly this machine was conceived. The plumbing team then demonstrated their invention by laying the tree trunk down on a wide beam. At one end of the beam was a spring loaded square plank that applied force on one end of the log toward the auger bit. The spring loaded square board pushed on the end of the timber which was forced against the tip of the auger. The donkey would walk in a circle harnessed to one end of a pole. On the other end of the pole was a series of gears that would then turn the bit as it carved its way the log's center mass. Different sized bits were changed out according to the needed center diameter of the hollow. The resulting inner diameter dictated which pile the new pipe was stacked onto. The system called for bigger pipes to feed an ongoing line of smaller and smaller openings delivering water to the necessary locations with pressure. At the end of the line the system connected to the sewage retrieval and disposal system.

The entire project was designed to use gravity and pressure to keep the water moving in and out at all times. At the end of the waterline the sewage removal system began and safely processed all the collected waste water back toward the top deck and then overboard into the ocean of floodwater. The ark then continued floating toward wherever God directed it. Noah's son Shem realized that an additional remedy was needed to prevent a potential plague. He stated "that the pipe that was continually siphoning the water into the system had to be placed on the starboard side. The pipe for sewage disposal overboard had to be placed on the port side. Thereby keeping the drinking water separate from the waste water," he explained. Everyone else immediately recognized the brilliance of this recommendation and installed it into the blueprint.

According to God's dictation to Noah, there was to be a door, a large door, in the side of the ark. "Should it be a double door that swings open on hinges from both sides and latches shut in the center when they meet in the middle? Perhaps it should be a single unit that has hinges along the bottom and falls open, forming a ramp as it hits the ground below," questioned Noah. The idea of utilizing the door to be a ramp for the animals to use in order to enter appealed to all of them. They never gave sufficient consideration as to how heavy such a door would be and whether they would be able to pull such a heavy platform back up in order to seal off the entryway.

According to their plans, the dimensions of the side opening had to be tall enough for the tallest animals to walk through and for the birds to fly through. It had to be wide enough to accommodate multiple animals passing through at once. A very important thing to address was the seal, it had to have an air tight connection to the door frame. They agreed to make it half the height of the ark, 25 feet tall. They also decided to place it on level with the middle floor. They made this decision so that no animal had to walk more than one level to reach their own shared cages.

"The animals will certainly come, Noah assured them all. This is not in vain. The animals will arrive in pairs, two and two, male and female each pair, only. God was very clear about this, He will bring them at the right time, when we are ready for them, but not before then. Male and female, they will come to us and we will keep them and their seed alive upon the earth," he exclaimed.

"Let's combine two subjects of conversation into one event, said Shem. All this talk of animals at lunch time is making me very hungry. What do you all say we take our midday break now and tackle both issues at once?"

"I second that motion," his wife quickly replied.

At the family meal that followed the topic of animal locations and the lay out of the animal housing on each level rose for discussion. Everyone understood that they could not just let thousands of wild animals roam freely throughout the vessel at sea. They had to be contained. The use of cages for that purpose was an obvious choice as a solution to that issue. What about the layout though? Asked one of the wives. "Where will we put all those different kinds of animals so that it is most beneficial to them and to us since each floor will have its own unique setting and feel to it," she finished? "This issue also must be contemplated further," agreed Noah.

"The lowest level will no doubt be the darkest of all the floors, they presumed. The light that enters through the windows on the top floor will certainly not penetrate to the bottom floor. Essentially, the only way to see down there will be with a handheld torch, either carried or temporarily hung in a wall socket. Nevertheless, the location will be conducive to animals that enjoy such a setting," they agreed. Additional information provided by Ham was that "the bottom level will exist below the water level as the ark floats along. This could possibly resemble the feeling of living under ground. Reptiles would most likely be well at ease on that floor." All of the wives agreed at that moment that the bottom floor will indeed be the best place for the snakes and other scaly and crawling animals. "As far away from us as possible," they finished.

The second, or middle, floor will have much more illumination by contrast. It would also be the loudest level having access to sound vibrations from below and above it at all times. It will be conveniently located, however, being the level with the entry door and easily accessible from anywhere on the ship.

The family was going to live on the top level. Each son was going to have his own living quarters with his wife. "The quieter animals that tend to be more easily domesticated ought to be the ones to reside on that level with us," said Naamah. Of course, no one could predict how many animals there would be or the sizes of them when they arrive. They trusted God and their father that the given dimensions for the project would prove sufficient for any and all needs. Would the animals that arrive be young or full grown and capable of reproduction? For animals like mice this was not an issue but for large live bearing animals even their babies can be large.

What exactly did God mean when He told Noah, "the animals will come to you?" Noah admitted that he neglected to ask God any specific questions or get details on the matter. "That's ok, there will be many things that we will have to adjust to and accommodate for regularly," the family assured him. They decided to just leave those details for God to work out and focus on the ones that they can control.

Containers for the large variety of animals that certainly will board the ship also needed their attention. Birds did not require the same accommodations as cattle. Snakes would never remain confined within a standard barred cage. "There needs to be a place for each type which would be right for them," Noah's wife concluded. Noah reminded everyone, "we have worked with all types of animals in all kinds of settings and situations on our ranch. Keep in mind that we know how to work with them and how to provide care sufficiently for each in order to increase in numbers. Let's rely on our expertise in this area."

"Not all animals will need to be fed and watered with the same routine. While many would require daily attention and maintenance, not all will. Most importantly none of the animals can perish on the voyage to the new and unknown world," he continued.

"There certainly can be no deaths among them due to our own mishandling of them, neglect or improper care. This rebuilding and repopulation project simply cannot afford a single loss. Ultimately, our faith has to be in God to remember us all and to bless each one on the ark in order to keep their seed alive," Shem said.

Japheth then stood up in front of them, "So then, there is yet one last thing for us to construct. One last subproject that requires attention: the building of the cages. Since we are very accustomed to animals as well as their needs and tendencies in many different situations let's not fret about this most important project. Remember, all animals act differently when under stress than they do when they feel secure. A familiar surrounding renders a different response from them than an unknown and uncertain setting. Due to the very nature of our upcoming journey being one of turmoil and upheaval, let's estimate that our ward's reaction will be one of stress. To give them a large nest area would be counterproductive and potentially harmful. They would best be suited in a small enclosed structure within the ark. An assortment of barred cages, hanging enclosed baskets, ventilated clay pots with lids, and small boxes coated with pitch has be built for each animal according to their need."

The locations where each cage will be located was beginning to come clear to them as well. The reptiles must be housed in the bottom level for obvious reasons." The wives simultaneously let out a cheer at hearing that decision. He continued, "they all respond well to dark, chaotic environments by naturally going into an inactive state. While in that state they generally do not move, hunt, eat, drink, or make waste. They are happily suited to remain in that condition for long stretches of time. This realization would alleviate a lot of the pressure of caring for all on board. Snakes, lizards, alligators and crocs, turtles, frogs and other scaly types would live in the dark moist bottom level.

It would be the most difficult level in which to do the work that must be done but the amount of work and length of time required to complete it will be much less. Those sleepy and lethargic tenants have many fewer needs than those residing on the other two floors. "Halleluiah," the women said again.

The snakes would be placed in covered earthen pottery and placed along the walls. The larger reptiles would be in cages grouped in the center of the floor. Turtles and frogs will dwell in boxes containing some moist soil and insects with them for food. Most of these animals will be capable of going extended lengths of time without eating much at all. We must regularly tend each one according to a schedule."

Noah added, "the second level will be the middle deck where the entrance into the ark will be located. On one side of the floor will be a ramp that descended into the bottom level. Across the room from that ramp will be an ascending platform that will rise into the first floor. The top level will be the place where we will reside in our quarters. From there we will be able to look out of the windows and see the watery world and all its changes each day." As the planning session continued it was decided that the top floor will also be the location where all of the fowl will be housed. "Cages will need to be hanging from the top rafters and each one will contain a male and female bird. Every crossbeam will have many cords hanging from them from which each cage will dangle. The cages must be light but sturdy, made from bamboo shoots, twigs and branches which will be woven into a sphere shape. Be sure to put a hinged door for an entrance. We will also need larger containers that will rest on the floor. These will be for the walking birds that cannot fly. Some of them might be quite large. Their nesting material has to be supplied for each pair in order to accommodate for their own comfort and tranquility." Noah and his family realized that if the women will leave the cage doors open when the birds arrive that they would naturally fly or walk into a container of their choosing. Shem's wife compared what they expect to their regular experience on the estate, "like the birds that have always been on our farm, each pair will claim their own preferred location." The wives then volunteered to remain on the top floor come that future day so as to close the cage doors once the occupants entered them. "We can't allow any territorial battles to occur so we must get to each cage quickly and close each door upon the occupant's arrival," Naamah said. "This will have the desired effect of eliminating battles between the different varieties," Ham's wife agreed.

They continued, "the entry level is going to be where most of our day to day activities will take place. The four legged animals, large and small, must live there. The bigger animals' cages will have to be placed in the center of the floor. The smaller cages will be in rows along the sides of the walls. The placement of the bars of the bamboo cages will be placed in relation to each other depending on the size of the intended occupants. The entry door of each cage must be made according to the size of the animals expected to live in the cage as well. "We do not want a small animal in a huge enclosure, said Shem's wife. Our plan is to have small animals pick the smaller cages and large animals in the bigger cages. For birds and animals the door size would naturally help the selection process, they anticipated, and help prevent a need for most of our relocation efforts."

The family anticipated that "most of the incoming water should be directed from the top level to the second level for drinking and waste removal. The animals on that floor will not hibernate or slowdown in biological requirements or processes like the reptiles will. As a result of their daily needs the residents on the middle level will require a constant, reliable source of water for drinking and sewage removal every day that they live there." This, everyone expected, will not be a problem, however, because the siphoning valve on the intake line will enter the ark at the top level and gravity feed to the lower levels from there.

"The sewage disposal pipe will exit the vessel from that middle deck on the opposite side of the water intake line. This will keep our drinking water safe."

Once again everyone was glad to hear these plans, each person understood how important they are and everyone was relieved to know that the water issues will not become a problem. The water and sewage systems were carefully engineered for success. The water containment method was also systematically manufactured. Everyone was confident that any potential problem concerning individual water needs will never materialize.

The last subject that was discussed at the meal was Grandpa Methuselah. The woman were the unchallenged experts concerning this topic. Each day the wives spent many hours helping Methuselah get back to health. Shem's wife stated that she expected him to be spry enough to take his normal place at the family meals in a few more days. The family members cheered when they heard that news. They were genuinely happy for him but they also knew what is going to happen shortly after his passing. *We are not ready yet for that to happen*, thought Noah.

She continued with her report: "a few days ago his fever was very high. I struggled to get it down to a safer level. He began to speak of events and people from long ago. It reminded me that he was a contemporary of Adam and he knew him well. Grandpa spoke on as if I was not even in the room. He looked right past me. He described the coming flood, the Lord's coming and the end of the world as we know it. I couldn't believe what he was saying. His eyes were open, but he was not seeing through them. He spoke like he was talking to a group of students. The earth will tremble and shake violently. The deep will be torn apart and the flood waters will burst through their restraints as they climb rapidly to the surface. Higher and higher they will rise, she repeated, for days on end. There will be no place for them to go. The people, Nephilim, and the animals will struggle in futility against the ever-rising tide. They will cling, claw, scratch, grasp and finally cry out to the God Whom they mocked their entire life. Most will be swept away; in an instant they will be gone. There will be smaller groups that will evade the crashing rivers that will be rolling over the hills. They will face their end as the water pulls them all under. Their struggles might continue with their heads barely above the tempest for a short period.

Everybody and every living thing will perish, finally silencing their screams and cursing. All flesh will sink to the watery bottom far below them. The rain also will come down from the sky. Great layers of water will fall hard. Down they will pour from the firmament and fall for 40 days and 40 nights. The world will be buried beneath the water and nothing will remain except us, the ark and the animals on it. There will be no land above the surface anywhere on the earth, as we float along for months on end," she finished.

As she concluded each family member just stared at her. No one could release themselves from the gripping scenes of horror that were vividly painted in their minds through her descriptions. Even Noah couldn't say anything for moments. Finally, he said, "God be praised for His great mercy to us and for His righteous judgements upon the wicked. The Seed will prevail, His salvation will come. The earth will see His glory and be renewed again," he concluded.

CHAPTER NINE

F inally, the men could visualize what they were building and began to clearly see the formation of the frame and structure of the ark.

The first thing that was built was the enormous and long keel. Once that was completed, they began framing the vessel by tying the framework into the keel and running it all the way up the sides of the hull. Then they tied the huge upright stanchions into the horizontal beams that ran along the bottom of the hull. These beams would also serve as a subfloor along the bottom of the ship, upon which the floorboards would eventually be placed. The outer walls continued to progress upward from keel to captain's quarters and on up to the top roof. The various types of flooring were also added as the pre-planning dictated.

A trough was installed in the center of each floor from bow to stern where a continuous strong and steady course of water could flow. All the animal waste was to be broomed into the fast-moving stream each day and then the system would carry it to the end of the trough and into the elimination chamber. Once in there the contents would be quickly sucked out by the siphon pressure and dispersed overboard through the discharge pipe.

Their construction plan involved building the ark from bottom to top. After they constructed a floor the crew built up the side walls until they reached the level where the next floor was to be laid. As the men moved from building the bottom floor up to the middle level the external shell of the hull made its way upward toward the top. Finally the top floor was also finished and the ark was taking the shape of a water tight life container.

The women also began to see that their monumental task of food collection and preparation was also really coming together. Beyond simply preserving large quantities of food they also had to prepare it and devise different storage methods for it. The need for food was going to last for as long as they remained in voyage. The wives calculated that they needed to prepare for that necessary supply of food the entire time that it took for the men to construct the ark.

The "food committee" also made great progress in specializing their food preparation and storage venture. Each day they focused their efforts on a particular food source and devised various ways to prepare, preserve and store it. Vegetables and meat could be preserved in a number of delicious ways. They pickled, cured, smoked, salted, dehydrated, canned and used a variety of cooking methods to safeguard their long-term human food supply. For the animals the women stored, canned, stocked, warehoused, compressed, and bundled different grasses, foliage, roots, barks, and grains. They also set up a system where animal proliferation would be used as a meat source for the meat-eating animals. Rabbits, varmints, mice, and reptiles could all bear excess offspring to be used for that purpose. Many of those animals breed more often in the course of a year as well. "Certainly, they concluded, the ark was not the place and the voyage was not the time to replenish their numbers, so we might as well plan on benefitting our cause from nature," said Japheth's wife.

There was no shortage of expertise, wisdom or resources in their group. They just did not know how many animals would eventually arrive or how long they would have to feed them. For these uncertainties they made sure there was too much stored food so that they would be sure to have an abundance during the entire journey to the new world.

ELLIPSIS

Noah's wife was a stickler for detail, she even kept a book of her own. She made sure to count, weigh, measure, and sort every bit of provision. She kept a ledger and inventory sheet to ensure long range planning and the project's success. "Nobody is going to starve or get hungry," she said. Many times she was seen with hers and Noah's books in her hands, bringing his out to him in the construction yard. "Make sure you keep record of all this, honey," she would say to him. "Don't leave silent gaps in the record of God's history among His people. The Seed is coming and your writings will continue the eternal testimony of the events used to usher Him here," she continued.

Noah immediately knew that his wife was right, he saw that she was diligent to keep her own book. He realized that he had been neglectful of late of his most sacred duty. A stab of remorse pricked his heart and he felt a wave of heat come over him. Noah immediately felt as if he let his most precious Friend down when he was needed the most.

"Thank you dear, he replied, I shall endeavor to be more conscientious each day regarding this matter." "That's alright love, she said, I'll bring it out to you tomorrow too, if you need me to." They both laughed together about that.

He gently took the book from her outstretched hand and went to ask Shem, Ham, and Japheth to excuse him from work for the rest of the day if need be. His sons, seeing what has come over their father, easily consented. "Sure dad, take all the time that you need," they replied.

With the archive tucked under his arm he withdrew from their sight so that he could tend to this weightier matter. When Noah reached his isolation, he began in prayer: "most holy God, You have been so good to me. You have saved me and my loved ones from the coming destruction. You crowned our efforts with success. The ark is being built and will be complete soon. It has taken a lot of preparation and work which has had an effect on me. You have been faithful to strengthen us but I have not been faithful to You as I should have been. I know that You are saving us to keep the seed alive upon the earth. Some day and soon the Seed of the woman will come and crush the serpent's head because You saved this remnant. Help me be more faithful to You and to keep my priorities in order. Amen."

Instantly he felt layer after layer of pressure fly off of his entire being. *I feel like I just received a healing,* he thought. He had been so used to the press of the urgency of fulfilling his call and the weight that it put upon him. He didn't even realize that he was so burdened. He just thought *tremendous feelings of stress are normal.* From that moment of relief Noah was determined to be more reliable with being the keeper of the Truth as revealed in the sacred passages. *It has been passed down through the lineage and I will not fail in my part either,* his thoughts continued. *Some day I too will relay it onto one of my sons. I must impress upon each of them about the critical nature of that essential work as it was impressed upon me long ago.* He privately hoped that the heir of the duty would soon be revealed.

Hours later Noah returned to the work site and watched as a stranger was running away from them into the path through the distant trees. Upon his approach his wife looked at Noah with tears in her eyes. "Who was that?" he asked. That was a messenger sent to tell you that your father, Lamech, had just died. You might want to go to see them.

"Let the dead bury their own dead", he replied. "I must be about my God's business."

Darkness was upon them, so they called it a day and went home to commemorate a life well lived in Lamech.

The men had been working on this project for so long. All of the manual, physical labor was taking its toll on the workers.

The death of Lamech was a final blow that put Japheth into anguish, "Why are we doing all of this? We still have a long way to go. It is going to take five more years to put everything together and finish the ark. If God wants to destroy all of the corruption and evil in the world, why bother to spare us?" Noah insisted to his son, "there is inherent value in man as he was created, man is made in God's image and is so much more valuable than we suppose. God has a plan which will be fulfilled and a pure and spotless group that are called and separated just for Him that love Him. That is His desire. The Seed will come! His plan will be fulfilled. He will stomp the head of the wicked one and all will be glorious. We are being preserved as part of that plan. He will bring this all to a victorious end where there is no sorrow, no death, and no shifting shadows of evil. That time has not come but we must prepare so that what you desire can be realized, son."

Lamech was 777 years old when he died. His father Methsuselah was much older than him and he was still alive. "How much longer will he live?" They wondered. This realization caused the family to take stock in their progress on the ark's construction. They knew of the old time prophesy concerning Methuselah and the destruction to come at his end. "We were so close to losing him that day he was so fevered. That was way before we are ready, Naamah said, you men have no idea just how close we were. God really did answer our prayers." They were all reminded, once again, and were aware that Methuselah already lived longer than any other person in history. Noah read to them all about this from the historical record. They also knew what his name means and why Enoch had given him that name. "When he dies, the deluge." *Such a long time ago those words were spoken over him as a lad, how long will it be till they're fulfilled?* They renewed their resolve to work on the ark with a single definiteness of purpose.

Time continued to pass. The pitched boards were nailed into the pitched framing which was secured to the keel which was covered with pitch. Pitched beams, ribs, and stanchions were firmly fastened with tree nails that were coated with pitch. As the hull rose toward the top of the ark, the floors were finished off too. Although they all felt an urgency and a push to complete the task, they still put a professional artisanship into their handiwork. Some of the wood structures that they created were strikingly beautiful. They would serve as the only link and a memory between the old world and the new one to which they were going. "In the years ahead, said Noah, everybody who sees this ark and the handiwork of the wood, will know that not everything in the old world was dark and ugly. This beauty will be a testimony to God's love for whoever sees it."

Of course the book was going to be on the ark as well and Noah intended to select his eventual successor at some point after they arrive in their new home, *when the situation presents itself,* he thought.

Finally all three dwelling levels were completed and the pitched roof was installed. The men still had to do the finishing work on the air ventilation system. "This will provide the necessary air supply and circulation for the crew and passengers, said Shem. With a system of windows which were installed a cubit from the ceiling there will be a cross ventilation of flowing air. In addition to that, these air vents were installed directly under each window. The vents will catch the incoming air and the cool breezes will naturally travel downward through the shafts and into the lower levels of the ark. Large floor grates were placed along the walls of each floor to allow for a warm air return to the top in order to complete the air cycle."

With ventilation, plumbing, sewage, and a water tight vessel built to God's dictated specifications, I believe that we can all be extremely confident in our eventual success once the journey begins," congratulated Noah.

Japheth remarked, "Where there once was an uncountable number of stacks of boards, and building supplies in a homemade lumber yard, there is now an ark that is visible for what it is. It is a spectacle to behold. There in the middle of dry ground, far from any sea is the largest structure that had ever been built. Let the mockers say what they want to about it for now. So long forever, will be our response soon."

"That is true, replied Shem, the preservation of the Seed will make it all worthwhile. Let's not begrudge the unbelieving mockers."

"Doesn't it strike you as being very strange that even with this massive structure being completed in their midst that not one in that entire crowd ever considers the possibility of the flood or their own destruction? Said Noah. They continue to go about living their lives as if God does not exist and they are going to live forever and never face the Judge."

"At the beginning of this project the coming flood was what motivated me to do the work, now with this ark being plain to see, it should do the same for them. They should all know to repent," replied Shem.

Repent?" Asked the local onlookers. "These people are crazier than we ever thought they were," others said.

The crowd of gawkers was growing by the day. It was fast becoming a throng. To the family it seemed that the crowd was growing in multitude by the hour. Most of them were there to spectate and to speculate as to the reason for such a foolish enterprise. More than a few of the opportunistic ones sold tickets to the tourists for a chance to stand in the best locations. "From here you can see the crazy builders and be close enough to heckle them so they'll be able to hear you," said one advertisement. "There is no water anywhere near here, Noah, you must have water on the brain they yelled." The crowd laughed at every taunt. Noah knew that they didn't believe God, neither would they believe him. He just kept pounding in his nails. They thought it strange that he never responded to their verbal jabs and criticisms. He did, however, answer them with his hammer. The pounding, pounding sound of their hammers preached of sin and judgment. Each coated tree nail that held the planks together in the construction of the ark was also speaking of the world's upcoming judgement of their sin and death. The construction sounds seemed to be saying, although without words, "everyone will either be in or out, there will be no middle ground, each person must choose what their future will be."

It was just a matter of a short time now. There were fewer and fewer things to be prepared on the ark before it is complete. "The next job will be packing everything onto the ark and then wait for their guests to arrive," the women agreed.

"It is time to load all of the food," Noah's wife told her daughters in law. Noah overheard her and began to consider the food relocation, as possibly, the biggest, most important job that was still left to do. "The warehouse is full of stored food and it all has to be relocated," she said to the men.

In order to do that Noah gave the command to, "drop the side door down so that we can use the carts to wheel the food up the ramp and into the storage area." "I will get the teams of oxen together and the biggest wagons that we have so that we can load them up and pull the carts into the designated areas within the ark. It is going to take a few weeks to get all the food that is in the warehouses into the ark," said Ham.

The crowd of onlookers watched the transfer of the supplies taking place, they figured out, "that those crazy people are going to live in that huge barge looking thing." Someone yelled out to Noah, "hey Noah, since you are moving why you don't give me a good deal on the purchase of your estate?"

Noah heard that comment and started to think. *When we leave here we will never come back to this place. We should sell it. We will not need this property or be anywhere near it wherever we land. I should sell it now and hire some town people to assist us in moving the supplies. If possible we can even buy more food off of them.*

When he introduced this plan to the other members of the family they all thought, "That idea makes perfect sense. By the time we get out of that ark, some day, we will have the whole world to ourselves. The choice property which is now owned by Kings will be available to us for the taking. We will not be needing our land anymore." So they sold.

Prior to the actual sale the family discussed that price was not as important as the timing of the sale and terms allowing them to separate the house, construction area and the ark from the rest of the estate. These things were not to be included in the estate sale. The rest of the land was the only thing considered for sale and that did sell quickly. Noah and his family maintained the essential property in the family name. He was very pleased with how they planned to use the money to finish the entire job.

Finally, there was a moment of reprieve from all the hectic activities so Noah and his wife went to visit his grandfather. "We haven't seen or heard from him in the past couple of days," she said. "Yes, lets fill him in regarding all of the latest transactions," he replied. Upon arriving at Methuselah's abode both Noah and Naamah were excited to tell him of the latest transaction and completion of the ark. "Now that you are back up and on your feet you need to come see how far we have gotten. We need your help in organizing the food storage, the animal's locations and other last minute preparations," she said.

"Let me get my sandals from the back room and then I will be ready to go," he replied. The husband and wife noticed a look of apprehension on Methuselah's face as he turned away. "He knows he is not going with us, that he will be dying very soon," Noah whispered.

Methuselah quickly returned with an uplifted demeanor. "I have long desired this day, to see God's salvation and to reunite with my father Enoch. Although I will soon be gone it will not be as an unbeliever but as the harbinger to the world now and forever," he said.

As they arrived back at the ark all three family members quickly noticed two young lions standing in front of the door of the ark as if they were waiting to be let in. Noah yelled ahead to his son, "is that a male and a female?"

Shem responded, "it is, and while my wife and I were in the fields today we observed that the animals throughout the area are on the move. We watched as wild and domestic animals alike gathered in groups as if they are being rounded into herds. We stared in amazement at their synchronized movements, then we saw a powerful looking angel causing the scene," he said.

Shem's wife added, "Oh yes, we saw him. A large and powerful angel, skillfully separating the herds and taking two young ones from each type of animal, male and female. The older animals of the herds didn't even react to the taking of their offspring, it was so amazing."

Methuselah listened intently and replied, "hmm, I won't have time to eat today. We need to get on board to get started organizing and caging the animals correctly. We are going to be very busy."

Noah nudged Naamah to look into the horizon. "Here they come, she said, so many animals are heading this way. They are coming from every direction," she exclaimed.

As the day turned into evening the animals did not stop coming. At times the line to enter the ark backed up into the woods beyond the house. Methuselah worked energetically to supervise all three levels on the ark and to assist the women as they managed each floor. It didn't take very long for the four of them to get their efforts systemized and working very efficiently. "There are so many animals, said one wife as she looked outside at the lineup, it is going to take days to cage them all. Even with all of our experience there are just so many more than we have ever worked with at any one time in our lives."

"It is a good thing that their arrival is somewhat staggered and we are caging them as fast as they arrive, answered Methuselah. If we keep working at a steady pace we will be just fine, don't worry. If some of them have to spend a night or two outside the ark that will be fine. They all seem to be the young of their kind. They are not aggressive or diminutive yet, so they are all very predictable and much easier to handle." He knew that everything was in order. "The ark is complete, the food is prepared, the animals are here, Noah and his family are ready to go, and my time to die is at hand. I might not make it through this day, the Lord might let me finish placing the animals but maybe not, he told Naamah. I have had a very long and blessed life. So many have turned away from God and joined the line of the Nephilim but He has kept me pure. I am blessed and so thankful. I wish that I could go with you to the other world. Just to see it! That is what I have thought about my whole life and have prepared myself for this moment. It pains me to know that I cannot go with you but the Seed is safe now. The serpent and his Nephilim can't touch His line. His will be done in my life, blessed be the Lord."

Naamah began to weep as he discussed his life being at its end. It was a bittersweet moment for both of them. *We have worked and waited so long for this time and yet how we will miss him*, she thought.

The Lord gave the order: "go get him, it is time to bring judgement and salvation." Michael was dispatched to gather Methuselah's soul and usher him to the abode of God. "Methuselah was faithful as his father was, a general in My army. I am sending an archangel for him," God said.

As Methuselah was helping Naamah close the dove's bird cage his heart stopped beating and he fell to the ground. Naamah cried out for help but it was too late. There was nothing that anybody could do to bring him back. Methuselah was 969 years old and everyone in the family knew the prophecy about him. They all knew what was happening and why.

"We have to bury him and thank God for his life, said Japheth, but we must do it quickly." Ham asked his father if that was a good idea or not.

"We must respect the faithful departed, we owe him that," he replied.

While the wives were finishing up with the animals, the men dug a grave site just beyond where the latest arriving animals were standing. Noah's sons were obviously upset but not quite like they were after the death of Lamech. "I always knew that grandpa Methuselah couldn't go with us but I had hoped that grandpa Lamech would cross over to the new world with us, but it was not to be," lamented Shem.

While Noah was thanking God for His faithfulness and the

life of Methuselah the earth began to tremble. He and his sons could hear all of the mockers, who showed up daily, off in the distance as they cried out in terror. The ground shook and quaked lightly for a short time and was followed by a second tremor a few minutes later.

"What was that?" asked Shem. They would soon find out that many more were to follow and grow increasingly violent. "That was the beginning," answered his father.

As the men were finishing up their duties at the graveside God spoke audibly to them. "It is time for you and your wives to enter the ark. I have seen that you are righteous and faithful and have done everything that I commanded you to do. A few animals are yet to arrive at the ark. In seven days I will send the rain and the flood waters. I will cause it to rain for 40 days and 40 nights upon the whole earth. Every living thing that I made will be destroyed but you alone, along with your family and the animals with you on the ark will I save."

The men and women knew that the time was here and that everything they have done was going to be used to save them and the future of mankind both now and for eternity. Because of the ark and God destroying the work of Satan and the sons of Anak, the Seed will come and stomp the old Serpents head. Death will be defeated and life will reign forever.

QUESTIONS

Chapter One

1) Since the law had not yet been given concerning murder, how did Cain know others would be angry and seek vengeance if permitted?

2) Why was Cain's sacrifice not accepted by God? Why was Abel's accepted?

3) How did Abel's absence cause specific memories of Adam's failings in the garden?

Chapter Two

1) How would Abel have known about Eve eating the fruit?
2) Should Adam and Eve feel responsible for what happened to Abel?
3) Why would Cain lie about not intending to kill Abel?

Chapter Three

1) Why did they name their baby Seth, "the Lord replaces."
2) Do you think Eve truly was regretful of her actions all her life?
3) Do you agree with Seth's assessment about the importance of waiting for the right woman? Is this true for women as well?
4) Is Seth correct about the role of the husband/ father and their

job description?

5) Did you know that Jesus was prophesized about and referred to even in Genesis?

Chapter Four

1) What do you think people might have thought about Adam upon realizing the sin problem/ death originated with him?

2) Do you think Kennan made the right decision?

Chapter Five

1) Why was Enoch not scared of the Rephaim even while in their domain?

2) How were Enoch's government leaders similar to the government leaders in Jesus' time?

3) What does an occupation as an assassin say about the society?

Chapter Six

1) Do you think Methuselah should have abandoned his search?

2) What are some things that would make a prospective spouse unqualified for you?

3) Is it a good idea to involve family members in dating decisions?

Chapter Seven

1) If you were Methuselah would you have ended the boycott?

2) Do you believe God made certain people for success or failure?

3) How important is it to marry a servant of God?

4) Is there any scriptural basis for God's people having this much adversity from enemies?

5) Why did God specify the dimensions for the ark?

6) Does your family have meetings to discuss important matters?

Chapter Eight

1) Do you think Noah and his family gave a formula that if followed, will give a successful family?

2) Would it have been right for anyone to sit around and not work toward the completion of the ark?

3) How is building the ark similar to raising a family?

4) Do you think Noah and his family dealt with the hecklers the right way?

5) Is it a good idea to skip steps in order to get the job done faster?

Chapter Nine

1) Why did God send the flood?

2) Did Noah and his family trust God or just follow His commandments?

3) How did Noah and his family exemplify Philippians 3:13-14?

Name/lifespan	Yr. of birth	Yr. of death	Flood
Adam 930	0————————————————930		!
Seth 912	130———————————————1042		!
Enosh 905	235——————————————1140		!
Kenen 910	325————————————1235		!
Mahalaleel 895	395———————————1290		!
Jared 962	460————————————1422		!
Enoch 365	622————————987		!
Methuselah 969	687————————————————1656		!
Lamech 777	874——————————————1651		!
Noah 950	1056————————————2006		!

PROSPECTIVE ANSWERS
FROM THE AUTHOR

Chapter 1

1) Cain, like all people was made in the image of his Creator. Therefore, he had an inherent knowledge of good, and after the fall, evil. He was created with a conscience which convicted him in his thoughts any time after he did evil. Therefore, as his conscience accosted his mind he knew that what he did was evil and worthy of the death sentence. His concerns were soon confirmed by God that he was deserving of such a penalty but was to be spared.

2) Cain's sacrifice represented his attempts to cover his sin through his own efforts. He attempted to pay his debt to God with an offering that was not sufficient and he knew it. His parents were also rebuffed by God when they tried to cover their sin with handmade fig leaf garments. God instead slew an innocent lamb and with his sacrifice covered them with acceptable garments. The blood of an innocent lamb that was slain for the penitent sinner is God's only remedy. He was pointing to the sacrificial death of Jesus and our need to accept it as His only way.

3) Adam and Eve both knew that death entered paradise as a result of eating from the forbidden tree. The first death they experienced was separation from God, the second was physical

death which they had yet to experience but now experience it through their son.

Chapter 2

1) Adam and Eve were parents just like we have, had or will be. They talked to all their kids often about God and the need to get their life right with Him. Everyone on earth at the time was a direct descendent from them and had been raised with a knowledge of their experience which they shared in hopes of departing wisdom to their kids.

2) Adam and Eve were the ones that ushered sin into the world and the result of all sin is death. They were responsible and so perhaps took that fact into consideration in determining to banish Cain rather than execute him.

3) The authors presume that Cain lied about his intentions when confessing his crime to his parents and they suppose this to be plausible from reading Cain's interaction with God and rationalizing of his actions. He was hoping for a reduced sentence from them.

Chapter 3

1) The choice of Seth for the name of the newborn son represents their faith that God is merciful to comfort them in their loss and that the promised Seed will come. In deed Jesus is the Seed and did come through the line of Seth.

2) It is very likely that Eve was mindful and felt responsible for all that was going wrong in the world. She would certainly regret

her decision knowing that evil could have been avoided if she resisted the serpent at the tree.

3) The authors agree with Seth's assessment of the value to be placed on the decision to marry and who to marry. This decision brings with it many blessing to those who follow God's admonitions and pains to those who refuse them.

4) God has placed the man as head of his wife and family. There are many additional commands and examples given in the bible as to how to successfully function for the good and profit of the family and each family member.

Chapter 4

1) Surely Adam told his children about the events that happened in the Garden of Eden before, during and after the fall. This is the most reliable source of information about that time in history since there is no indication in the scriptures that God revealed the events to any prophet. As such Adam undoubtedly discussed those blessed days and the events of the fall to his children in hopes to guide them away from rebellion. If they held hostility and resentment toward him for the human condition or not can only be surmised. I suppose the people would have been as angry about it then as they are today, not much.

2) It is widely believed that not everybody is called to be in the ministry. Also, it is not everyone that is called for lifetime/fulltime ministry but can serve in that capacity during certain seasons of their life. To be sure, every believer is in the ministry by virtue of the fact that they are now children of God. Kenen continued his ministry away from the limelight and strife of the day in order

to devote his efforts in raising his family. Romans 14:22 Blessed is the man that does not condemn himself by what he approves.

Chapter 5

1) Enoch was a man of faith that had a very intimate relationship with God. No evil could befall him unless the Lord God ordained it to occur. In that case Enoch would gladly accept and endure any unpleasant event as that which his Father allows for his own good, no need to fear.

2) The government leaders in Enoch's time (according to this story) and Jesus' time (according to the gospels) were always planning and plotting ways to destroy them and kill them. Such is the way of all tyrannical governments where any threat to their hold over the people's thoughts and aspirations must be destroyed so they don't lose power.

3) Any society where its government leaders hire men to assassinate other men is sick and far from its God given purposes. Those who live in such a society might not be as safe from their government as they suppose themselves to be. History is replete with case examples of dictatorial governments wiping out individuals as well as entire populations within their society on a mere whim of the dictator.

Chapter 6

1) Methuselah was correct to eventually abandon his search for his father. The vision he experienced was convincing proof enough that he was never going to find or see him on earth again. He could have continued his search but it would have been in vain.

2) It is very important that the choice of who to marry be taken very seriously. That relationship is intended to be a lifelong blessing. If entered into lightly or without proper guidance and decision making process, the marriage relationship can cause lifelong regret, pain and bitterness for life.

3) Family members should be very interested in the wellbeing and important decisions of one. A great blessing comes from a family that looks out for the best interest of one another

Chapter 7

1) Methuselah was correct to hold strong until the end. The eternal salvation of his family was way more valuable than anything the Nephilim or this world could ever off. What does it profit a man to gain the world and lose his soul?

2) God desires everybody who trusts in Him to be successful. If you look to study and follow His commands and precepts, and apply them you are sure to progress more and more.

3) Beside surrendering your life to Jesus, the choice of who to marry is the second most decision one can make in this life. That is where many of the other blessings come from. It is very important to marry someone who already knows and serves the Lord. This decision should not be left to chance and blind hope.

4) Psalm 34:19 says: Many are the afflictions of the righteous, but the Lord delivers them out of them all.

5) The dimensions of the ark are the best and only reliable dimensions for a structural safe seaworthy vessel. That formula

given to Noah is still essential for today's ship builders: 30 to 5 to 3. (length to breadth to height)

Chapter 8

1) It used to be a common saying in America that "the family that prays together, stays together." There are certain activities and attitudes that promote family unity and success. Noah and Naamah had the right idea when they got the whole family involved and single minded toward a common goal where each member was valued and who's production toward that end was expected. Not everybody believed in what they were doing. The parents must have promoted the correct mindset in their children during their child rearing years.

2) You might be surprised to realize that people do this type of thing every day and throughout their lives. Those who believe in Socialism, for example, preach that those who do the work should have the fruits of their labor taken from them and given to those who did nothing to produce it. Were free rides offered on the ark to family members that wouldn't work? That scenario never arose. Maybe there is a connection between willingness to work and believing God.

3) Building the ark and raising a family are very similar in that they both require a commitment and devotion toward the stated objective. The commitment must endure through decades of progress and each member must be taught their skill and given opportunity to apply it for the good of others in the family. A selfish member that rejects the common goal and pursues their own ends does nothing to promote strong members or the unit.

4) Arguing with a fool seldom produces a change of heart in them that the wise man would like to see. Proverbs strongly counsels against answering a fool in the midst of their folly. Instead Noah and his sons gave an answer to each jab, joke, and jest with another board put in place and the sound of the next nail being pounded in. They were preaching of coming judgement for all who do not believe and change their lives to follow after God. When the water kept rising, I'm sure all the hecklers realized that they knew what the builders had been saying all along, they should have listened.

5) Simply stated the answer is NO. It is never a good idea to skip steps in order to finish the job faster. If you were charged with making a peanut butter and jelly sandwich and skipped a step or two in order to finish quicker, how would the sandwich taste?

Chapter 9

1) It is widely preached and believed that the only reason that God sent the flood was to punish the world inhabitants for their rebellion. Much of this is true but there is more to the reason for the flood than God's desire to deal out retribution. Throughout Genesis and in other Old Testament accounts there was a strong Nephilim population. Once they began cohabitating with humans the blood line through which the Seed must come would eventually become unsuitable for his advent. He could not be the son of Satan but had to be The Son of God. Therefore, through the flood the entire gene line of the Nephilim was destroyed and left only pure humans through who's lineage the Seed could come.

2) Certainly to undertake such a large assignment means that the family did trust God and this faith in Him prompted them

to follow the directions that no one else would. If they refused to build for some reason they would have been destroyed along with all the others. Would we be talking about their faith today? Following His commands and faith go together, they are the copper wire and electric current that gets the job done.

3) For all believers this principle is indispensable. We must release our past from us and surrender it to the Lord. As we live our lives, the eyes of our intentions and motivations of our hearts must be on seeking Him and becoming what He wants us to be through constant communion with Him.

CHARACTER MAIN EVENTS

Adam:
1)
2)
3)

Eve:
1)
2)
3)

Seth:
1)
2)
3)

Enosh:
1)
2)
3)

Kenen:
1)
2)
3)

Mahalalel:
1)
2)
3)

Jared:
1)
2)
3)

Enoch:
1)
2)
3)

Methuselah:
1)
2)
3)

Lamech:
1)
2)
3)

Noah:
1)
2)
3)

"ONCE YOU KNOW WHY, EVERYTHING ELSE MAKES SENSE."

CHRIS PAGANO

What were the people doing that was so evil in the days of Noah that caused God to send the flood? Was there a reason that God had favor on Noah and his family members and told them to build the ark to escape from the coming judgement? In their novel: The Battle For The Seed, The lost history and the saved race, Chris and Guy Pagano help the reader re-live those ancient times and discover what was going on everywhere on earth.

As a follow up to his first book: So Shall It Forever Be, The making of Satan, Pagano continues to weave biblical references from that time period to recreate the culture and popular trends of that era that ushered in the worldwide catastrophe.

Author Chris Pagano enjoys re-examining short biblical accounts and adding narration to those stories for the reader's appreciation. It is the authors' desire that this novel will add meaning to the sections in the Bible that many people simply skim over and just try to get through. It is their hope that the readers of this account will do as the Berean church and "search the Scriptures daily to see if those things were so ," after reading The Battle For The Seed.

BIOGRAPHY

Chris Pagano was born in 1963. He is the seventh child born in a large catholic family of eight children. Pagano earned a Master's Degree in education from Regent University and has 25 years of experience as a public school teacher. He also invests in property rentals and as a house "flipper." He is married to Alyce and has a daughter Hannah, and two sons Guy and Duncan. They attend church at Relevant Worship Center in St. Clairsville, Ohio.

Guytano (Guy) Pagano was born in 1998. He currently attends Ohio University Eastern and is majoring in business. Guy is planning on graduating in the spring of 2021 and becoming a realtor. After excelling in basketball through four varsity seasons and scoring over 1000 points he graduated high school in 2017. He went on to play basketball in college until two ankle surgeries ended his career. He then transferred to OUE and looks forward to beginning his career. This is his first authorship and he enjoyed creating this story with his dad.

www.ingramcontent.com/pod-product-compliance
Lightning Source LLC
Chambersburg PA
CBHW030310130626
46549CB00002B/795